No Ordinary Life

The True Story of a Dutch Girl and an American Marine

Paula Boswell

Wasteland Press
Shelbyville, KY USA
www.wastelandpress.net

NO ORDINARY LIFE:
The True Story of a Dutch Girl and an American Marine
by Paula Boswell

First Printing – July 2008
ISBN: 978-1-60047-224-4

This book is a work of non-fiction. Unless otherwise noted, the author and the publisher make no explicit guarantees as to the accuracy of the information contained in this book and in some cases, names of people and places have been altered to protect their privacy.

Printed in the U.S.A.

ACKNOWLEDGEMENTS

I want to thank my mother from the bottom of my heart for saving every one of my letters I wrote her from 1949—the year I left Holland—until 1982. She carefully put them in chronological order into three-ring binders. Whenever we sent postcards from trips, or when my husband or the children wrote her notes, they too found their way into the binders. Without those writings I couldn't possibly have remembered so many details of the life John and I shared for fifty-three years.

I will never be able to adequately thank my loving husband, John, for always standing by my side, wanting the best for me, and encouraging me in all my—at times crazy—endeavors throughout our married life.

I am equally grateful for the wealth of detailed information he left behind on growing up, joining the Marine Corps, and his forty months as a prisoner of war. Wherever he is now, I'm sure he is happy to know all his writings and research were not done in vain.

In my efforts to recreate his experiences I tried as much as possible to let John "do the talking," to quote his words verbatim. When I started to write these stories I knew he was looking over my shoulder, urging me on to tackle this new venture.

TABLE OF CONTENTS

Introduction   1

Chapter 1 – The Farm Boy   2
Chapter 2 – Marine Corps, the Early Years   9
Chapter 3 – War is Imminent   17
Chapter 4 – Prisoner of the Japanese   21
Chapter 5 – A Life-saving Beating   28
Chapter 6 – No End in Sight   30
Chapter 7 – Hell Ship to Japan   34
Chapter 8 – Slave Laborer for Mitsubishi   38
Chapter 9 – Post-war Years in the Marine Corps   44
Chapter 10 – Paula Growing Up   50
Chapter 11 – Holland under Nazi Regime   60
Chapter 12 – Tragedy Strikes   69
Chapter 13 – Is Liberation Near?   74
Chapter 14 – The Hunger Winter   82
Chapter 15 – Holland Is Free!   91
Chapter 16 – Hitchhiking   95
Chapter 17 – Nylon Stockings   97
Chapter 18 – A Failed Romance and Its Aftermath   99
Chapter 19 – Love and Marriage   103
Chapter 20 – Culture Shock   116
Chapter 21 – Mom Boswell and the Beast   120
Chapter 22 – The Ups and Downs of a Marine Wife   123
Chapter 23 – A Forced Separation   131
Chapter 24 – The Worst Place on Earth   137
Chapter 25 – Paula's Gift Shop   143
Chapter 26 – The Chandelier   149
Chapter 27 – Diamonds   152
Chapter 28 – San Francisco, Here We Come   155
Chapter 29 – A Dream Fulfilled   158
Chapter 30 – Camping   162
Chapter 31 – Wanna Buy A House?   167
Chapter 32 – My father, Paul van Dalsum   172

Chapter 33 – My Wonderful Mom   178
Chapter 34 – Bonifay Revisited   183
Chapter 35 – John the Teacher   186
Chapter 36 – My Sister Toto   190
Chapter 37 – A Late Bloomer   195
Chapter 38 – Thrift   202
Chapter 39 – A Hundred Dollar Windfall   206
Chapter 40 – Danville—One Acre Lot for Sale   208
Chapter 41 – A Family of Squatters   211
Chapter 42 – Mabel Kuss   214
Chapter 43 – The Start of a Business   218
Chapter 44 – Our Church Life   225
Chapter 45 – Heart Attack!   230
Chapter 46 – Once a Marine Always a Marine   235
Chapter 47 – The Veterans of San Ramon Valley   242
Chapter 48 – Forty Years of Marriage   247
Chapter 49 – The New Millennium   255
Chapter 50 – The Final Years   260
Chapter 51 – Going It Alone   268
Chapter 52 – Letters and Pictures   270

Epilogue   274

INTRODUCTION

This is the true story of two people growing up before World War II on opposite sides of the Atlantic Ocean. Their lives couldn't have been more different—John being raised as a poor farm boy in Northern Florida and Paula living in a seaside resort in The Netherlands.

Seeing no other way to assure a better future, John joined the Marine Corps at age seventeen. After a few years on a dream assignment in Shanghai, China, WWII broke out and his regiment was sent to the Philippines. Five months of fighting against hopeless odds followed, ending with the surrender of the entire U.S. Armed Forces on Bataan and Corregidor. On his twenty-second birthday John became a prisoner of the Japanese.

He survived the next forty months—more than 1200 days—in captivity under horrifying conditions. He defied certain death three times.

In 1940, at the other end of the globe, Hitler's mighty "Wehrmacht" invaded Paula's country. She lived what would have been her best teenage years under Nazi Germany's occupation and had her share of tragedy and deprivation. Keeping a diary during the "hunger winter" of 1945 contributed to Paula's recollections.

Five years after the end of the war John and Paula met in Lisbon, Portugal, fell in love, and started a life together. Their story, as told in this book, is interspersed with anecdotes about special people and events that affected their lives.

CHAPTER 1

The Farm Boy

"Watch out, there's a gator behind you!" someone yelled. John and his friends quickly scrambled out of *Gum Creek*, a muddy little stream that served as their swimming hole. The boys whooped and hollered as an alligator floated by, one of many such animals looking for prey in Florida's waterways.

Life wasn't always that exciting in Bonifay, a poor farming town in the Florida panhandle, midway between Pensacola and Tallahassee.

John Ray Boswell was born in that town on May 5, 1920. His parents, Florence and Ab (for Asberry), were 38 and 53 years old at the time of his birth. As was the custom in the area, boys went either by their initials or their middle name. John was called "Ray"; his three older brothers were named Columbus, J.D., and T.B.

John's dad owned a small farm. For their own consumption he grew fruit and vegetables, raised hogs and chickens and had a few milk cows. For a "cash crop" the farm grew peanuts and watermelons. In addition, Ab owned a syrup-making machine. Farmers from all around brought their sugarcane to be made into syrup, a procedure he had developed into a fine science, with varying amounts of sugar crystals and liquid—per request.

Their house was quite primitive; no indoor plumbing, gas or electricity. An outdoor pump supplied them with water while the rest of the "plumbing" consisted of an outhouse. Cooking was done on a wood-burning stove.

John loved the southern food his mother cooked: black-eyed peas with cornbread, southern-fried chicken with hushpuppies, collard greens and okra, and banana pudding or sweet-potato pie for dessert. Whenever the boys went squirrel hunting she made "smother-fried squirrel," a real delicacy according to John.

Luxuries were non-existent. They had no car, not even a bicycle. John, being the youngest, wore nothing but hand-me-downs.

John's father, a devout Christian, made sure the whole family attended the local Methodist Church each Sunday. What John remembered most about his dad was his integrity. He tried to instill principles of honesty and upright living in his boys at an early age. Once, when John was just a little boy, going with his mom to the grocery store, he got caught taking a piece of penny candy from an open bin. His dad lectured him: "You know, Ray, we may not have much money or other earthly possessions. But remember there's one thing of value that nobody can ever take away from you and that's *integrity*. Without that, your life will not be worth living."

Another time, while father and son were walking together on a dirt path, they observed two lizards mating. John thought it was funny and nonchalantly kicked them apart. "Don't ever do that again," his dad admonished him, "you don't disturb nature, you have respect for all creatures."

In Bonifay the boys had to invent their own entertainment. To play checkers they collected bottle tops, right side up for red and upside-down for black. They drew a checkerboard in the dirt.

John became an outstanding checker player; hardly anyone could beat him. Many years later he taught his strategy to his children and grandchildren.

When he was in second grade lots of warts mysteriously appeared on his hands. After trying various recommended salves without success, someone told him, "Go see the witch." Unbeknownst to John there was an old woman living on the outskirts of Bonifay who dispensed "magic potions," hence the name *witch*. After examining the warts she proceeded to give him an ordinary metal hairpin. "Now keep that pin in your hand all night," she ordered. John swore that after a few days all the warts were gone.

John and his three year older brother T.B. occasionally got into trouble. Once when T.B. had gotten hold of a pack of cigarettes he took his ten-year old brother aside: "Hey Ray, look what I've got. Let's go smoke them together." John was game. Soon there were puffing—and coughing—away out in the field, feeling like big shots. Their euphoria didn't last long. Suddenly they became aware of someone watching them. "Mother!" they cried out. Florence had caught them red-handed.

Her punishment was very imaginative. She bought a box of the cheapest, stinking cigars, took the boys outside and said, "Okay, you wanna smoke? Here's a whole box full. Don't stop until they're gone." Both of them got sick.

Another time the two decided to make rum from leftover cane syrup. They built a primitive still far out in the swamp and were well under way making bootleg rum. As the rum began to drip out, T.B. and John got so excited that they temporarily forgot to fan the smoke to disperse it. Ab saw smoke rising from the swamp and started to investigate what was burning. When he realized what his sons were doing, he kicked the still to pieces. The boys scattered in different directions. John was lost in the swamp for quite a while before getting home, where a good *whipping* was waiting for him. Whippings given by their father were administered with a belt, while Florence used a switch.

At age thirteen John reached his full height: 6'2". He quit high school during his junior year without opposition from his parents—they were only too happy to have an extra hand on the farm.

A few days a week he worked for a neighbor for $1 a day, cutting wood. After he had saved up a grand total of $5 he bought his first worldly possession—a guitar from a Sears Roebuck catalog. He taught himself how to play.

The house where John was born

John told several stories about growing watermelons. Once he and J.D. had marked the best looking melons in the field with a large X; those were to be kept out for seeds for the following year. One morning they noticed some neighbor boys in the field, who had picked a melon, cut it open and started to eat it. When John and his brother surprised them they apologized and said, "With so many melons in the field we didn't think eating one was a big deal." That's when John noticed the watermelon the boys were eating was marked with an X. Always ready to play a joke he said, "It's all right, as long as you don't take one with an X. They're poisoned to discourage theft." The boys quickly looked, saw the X and had a fit. They started to sweat and vomit and ran over to John's mother, asking for grease to drink to induce more vomiting. Even when John told them he was kidding, they wouldn't believe him and ran home screaming, "We're going to die, we're going to die."

Another story was less funny. In the year John turned seventeen Ab and his four sons prepared many acres to grow watermelons. They spent days plowing the grounds and laying out the rows. Next they put in the seeds, fertilized the grounds and hoed out the weeds and grasses. When the melons were ripe they harvested them, hauled them to the railroad station and loaded them into two boxcars. The melons were shipped to the New York market. A few weeks later they received a bill for the freight balance. The proceeds had not been enough to even cover all the freight.

That's when John knew with certainty he *did not want to become a farmer.* He decided the only way out of Bonifay would be to enlist in the Armed Forces.

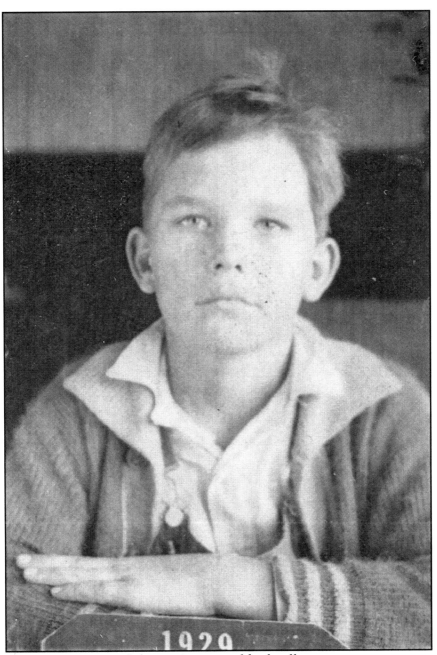

John as nine-year old schoolboy

John's parents in the late 1930s.
In the background a quilt made by Florence

CHAPTER 2

Marine Corps:
The Early Years

In August of 1937, at the age of seventeen with just a few dollars in his pocket, John hitchhiked to Savannah, GA to enlist in the Marine Corps. His decision to choose the Corps over other branches of the service was primarily based on the *uniform*—he loved those Dress Blues.

During the enlisting procedures a clerk asked, "Name?" He answered, "Ray Boswell." They checked a list and said, "Oh, there you are, John Ray Boswell. Okay, *John*, now go get your physical." From then on his name was John (or Johnny). The name *Ray* stayed in Bonifay.

The Marine Corps at that time set very high standards for acceptance. Of the twenty-five men in his group taking the physical he was only one of three passing. As John was "under-age" one problem remained, however. "We still haven't gotten permission from one of your parents," a captain told him. John had discussed his plans with his dad before he left Bonifay and knew how both parents felt; they unequivocally refused to give their consent. "I'll go home and get their signature," he assured the captain. John thumbed a ride to Bonifay, went to the Western Union office at the railroad depot and jotted down the words for a telegram to the recruiting officer: "My son John has my permission to join the USMC. Signed Richard A. Boswell."

9

Then he hitchhiked back to Savannah where he was told, "We've gotten your father's telegram. Welcome to the Marine Corps."

Having done heavy labor on the farm for many years, John found boot camp a breeze. He finished in October of '37 at the Marine Recruit Depot in Parris Island, SC.

While at his first duty station, the Navy Yard in Portsmouth, VA, he heard a lot of Marines talk about the fantastic duty in Shanghai, China. Being stationed there was rumored to be heaven on earth. Wanting to see far-away places, John asked for and got a transfer to Shanghai. In March of '39, before shipping out, he visited his parents. By that time they were resigned to John's departure from Bonifay. John would never see his father again.

A month later John left for Shanghai. He was now a PFC, one rank above private. Going up in rank in the Marine Corps was notoriously slow. In other branches of the service one could climb up in the ranks a lot faster. It didn't bother John; he was proud to be a member of what would later be referred to as the "Old Corps." Being in the Marines then was something very unique—the camaraderie among the men was exceptional. If you failed to adhere to their honor system you were unceremoniously dumped. John remembered how one of his bunkmates was "drummed out of the gate" for the theft of a single fountain pen.

The trip to China went via Cuba, through the Panama Canal and along the California coast to the Vallejo Naval Yard, about twenty miles from San Francisco. The ship went in dry dock for repairs for *thirty days*. The Marines took full advantage of this unexpected vacation. John wrote: *The World Exposition was held that year at Treasure Island, easy to get to from Vallejo on a ferry. Visiting San Francisco and Treasure Island was most enjoyable. The thought went through my mind that the Bay Area would be a nice place to live.*

From Vallejo the ship went to Hawaii, Guam and the Philippines. In July of 1939 John knew they were getting close to the China coast.

> *We saw more and more Chinese junks—flat-bottomed sail boats—and, as we neared land, harbor and river boats called sampans. Finally we headed up the Whangpoo River to the great city of Shanghai, one of the most beautiful and cosmopolitan cities in the world.*
>
> *Various odors wafted towards us—some pleasant, some not so. Then there were all the sounds: people shouting, and rickshaw coolies moving noisily through the crowds. Everywhere you looked were people, people, and more people.*

John became part of the 4th Marine Regiment, the "China Marines"—coveted duty! The Fourth Marines, according to John's writings, had to *look sharp, think sharp, act sharp and be sharp*, as they were observed by every major power in the world. They provided the only military force to counter Japanese territorial aspirations toward Shanghai, protecting life and property in the International Settlement. All areas outside the settlement were under Japanese control.

The new arrivals were informed that the "Fourth" wore tailor-made clothing, from boots to headgear. Tailors were meeting the Marines to take measurements. John, who had never owned a suit in his life, was now fitted for Dress Blues, civilian suits and regular uniforms. A cobbler guaranteed "no squeak" hand-sewn shoes and boots.

Money? No problem. Every Marine could sign a chit for credit, to be paid off in monthly installments. On arrival, John got *five* Chinese *yuan* for one U.S. dollar, but by the time the last payment on the new clothing was due the exchange rate was close to *thirty* to one.

Soon John started a life he had never known existed. Even as a lowly PFC he had more money than he ever dreamed of.

Located in the center of the International Settlement was the Fourth Marines' Club, considered by many the finest enlisted men's club in the world. It contained literally every amenity under the sun: bar, restaurant, soda fountain, recreation room, ballroom, library, bowling alley, gymnasium, and theater.

For additional fun and entertainment sports leagues were organized. John became an enthusiastic rugby player, participating in weekly games against British teams. The Marines published their own magazine, the "Walla Walla," which listed the results of all sporting activities in great detail. In the "gossip" column John's name was mentioned several times.

Since members of the 4th Regiment were allowed—and financially able—to live off base, John rented rooms at the home of a *White Russian* woman. There were a lot of White Russian families in Shanghai, refugees from Bolshevik—*Red*—Russia during the Russian Revolution a few decades earlier.

John had a Chinese servant, a *houseboy*, who polished his shoes, did his laundry and whatever else John needed, all on the salary of a PFC. That reminds me of a funny, true story. When it became known that officers' wives were allowed to join their husbands in Shanghai, John's CO, a captain, immediately sent for his wife. She arrived early one evening. The captain in his excitement had forgotten to inform his houseboy about her coming. The following morning he left for work, leaving his wife in bed, fast asleep. Not long after, the houseboy barged into the bedroom to make the bed. Upon seeing this strange woman, he shook her till she woke and said, "Get up, Missy, time to go home."

Over thirty-five years later John happened to run into his former CO—now a retired colonel—in the PX on Treasure Island and discovered he and his wife lived only five miles from our home. They had been lucky enough to catch the very last ship home from Shanghai. The four of us became good friends.

As was to be expected, John didn't want this dream assignment to end: *I soon learned to love Shanghai. The duty was good! The exchange rate was good! The social life was good! So I extended my tour of duty and waved goodbye to my friends who left on the ship I would have taken had I not extended my tour.*

Soon after, John was chosen by Major Lewis "Chesty" Puller to be the American flag bearer in the weekly parades. Major Puller (later a three-star general) was the Marines' executive officer, who took personal charge of "showing off the flag." They paraded through the streets in their immaculate, tailor-made uniforms, illustrating the Americans weren't intimidated by the Japanese. The Chinese loved the parades but were even more grateful for the security the Marines brought. They lined the streets to cheer the men on.

Many Chinese had fled, often with just the clothes on their back, to the International Settlement in order to escape Japanese aggression and brutality. Some lived in huts in the slums, without sanitary facilities. The "not so pleasant" odors John had observed on entering Shanghai came from the "honey carts," hand-pushed carts collecting human waste door to door in the slums. When filled to capacity the carts were taken to ships that dumped the sewage far out at sea.

There were a lot of Chinese beggars on the street, some just small children. They had learned to say in English: "No Mama, no Papa, no chow chow," while holding out their hands for a few pennies. John and his friends got a kick out of those kids and thought they could do better with a more elaborate *spiel*. A short while later the children sang: "No Mama, no Papa, no chow chow, no motor car, no whiskey soda, no Russian girlfriend, I'm so sorry for myself." This new version greatly increased their handouts.

Sadly, John's enviable life was not to last. War was raging in Europe. With the Japanese and the U.S. on a collision course, the International Settlement became very dangerous. Roosevelt ordered the 4th Marines, about 750 men in all, to depart for the Philippines. At the end of November 1941 the *China Marines* marched for the last time through town, accompanied by the 4th Regiment band. They boarded the *President Madison*, sailing towards an uncertain future. They were leaving *heaven* behind and were entering the gates of *hell*.

John in tailor-made uniform

Enjoying the good life in Shanghai

CHAPTER 3

War is Imminent

John's regiment was transported from Shanghai to Olongapo Naval Station in the Philippines. A little over a week later, on December 7, the Japanese attack on Pearl Harbor neutralized the U.S. Pacific Fleet, which resulted in declaration of war with Japan by President Roosevelt. That same day, just ten hours later, Clark Field, near Manila, was bombed, eliminating the U.S. Air Force in that part of Asia. The defenders of the Philippines found themselves fighting a land war without naval or air support. In other words, they were doomed from the start.

After severe bombing raids on Olongapo, General MacArthur ordered the Fourth Marine Regiment to the island of Corregidor, "The Rock," to set up beach defense. The men made a stopover on Bataan, where they were served Christmas dinner: stewed tomatoes with "hard tack,"—a dog-biscuit type cracker—a far cry from their lavish, seven-course meal just a year earlier in Shanghai. The Marines didn't know it then, but they were the lucky ones; by being ordered to Corregidor they avoided the horrific Bataan Death March.

Corregidor was a tadpole-shaped islet, slightly over four square miles in area, at the entrance of Manila Bay, a few miles south from the Bataan Peninsula. The hilly island was divided into three strategic parts, each with their own barracks: Topside, Middleside, and Bottomside. Underneath the island lay the

Malinta Tunnel, a massive, bombproof tunnel complex. Besides serving as MacArthur's headquarters and storing food and ammunition, it contained a 1000-bed hospital.

John was billeted in Middleside, a very long— nicknamed *mile long*—three story concrete building. Coast Artillery personnel already stationed there assured the new arrivals they had nothing to worry about, as Middleside Barracks were bombproof and the Japanese would never bomb Corregidor.

On 29 December 1941, the Marines were settling into the barracks, awaiting assignment to beach defense. Suddenly the air alert sounded. Orders were shouted to move to the lowest floor at once. Not only were Japanese planes bombing Corregidor, but the first bomb to hit Middleside Barracks penetrated all three floors, exploding at ground level, killing several men. Immediately after the alert stopped John and his buddies were told to assemble their gear and prepare to move out to their assigned beach defense areas. "H" Company, of which John was a member, was assigned to *James Ravine*. John remembered: *I was impressed with the beauty of the land. The area around James Ravine was like a park—tropical trees and lush vegetation throughout. It was truly lovely!*

Around the beach the land was very rocky, which made digging foxholes and tunnels tough. For days you could hear the sound of axes, pecking away at the rocks, as the men were trying to dig as deep into the ground as possible, anticipating what was to come.

Bataan surrendered on April 9, 1942. John, through his binoculars, seated in his foxhole, could actually observe the beginning of the Bataan Death March. Two days after the fall of Bataan, MacArthur left for Australia. Before his departure he issued a bulletin to the troops, saying, "Help is coming. Hundreds of ships with food and ammunition, as well as thousands of men are on the way." Alas, these were empty words.

It came to light after the war that the Pacific Front had been written off from the start by the U.S. War Department. America simply didn't have enough resources to fight in Europe and Asia simultaneously.

> *By mid April our food rations had become pretty meager. For several months we had received meals only twice a day and even those were mediocre at best. I figured I had lost at least twenty-five pounds since leaving Shanghai.*
>
> *The heavy bombardments by the Japs, which were a daily occurrence, often resulted in army mules being killed. At night our butchers salvaged anything edible. Our two meals a day improved until the meat ran out.*
>
> *Japanese attacks became more and more intense; bombings and shellings seemed endless. Inevitably we suffered many casualties. One day a grenade hit my good buddy, Bob Martineau, shattering his left leg. To keep him from bleeding to death he needed medical help at once. Brave corpsmen, in danger of their own life, crawled through the battlefield to administer first aid and to take him to the hospital in the Malinta Tunnel.*

John heard much later that Bob's leg had to be amputated. As the hospital didn't have his—somewhat rare—blood available, an urgent call went out among the fighting men for a donor. A tall, gangly man, nicknamed "Skinny," volunteered. Bob's life was saved.

By now the Marines knew that their actions were futile. While the Japanese military had the latest in modern equipment and a seemingly endless supply of fresh, well-trained troops, the Americans were fighting with rusty, outdated weapons of WWI vintage. No replacements for the worn-out men, no new weapons, ammunition and food were forthcoming.

General Wainwright, who was left in command after MacArthur left, realized the hopelessness of the situation. Against orders from Washington to fight till the bitter end he surrendered the entire Armed Forces in the Philippines when the Japanese invaded Corregidor, thus avoiding total annihilation.

The invasion happened on May 5, John's 22nd birthday. Several of his friends teased him: "Johnny, we know you like fireworks on your birthday, but this is too much!"

As for the former beauty of the island, in just a few short months Corregidor had been reduced to an utter wasteland.

It wasn't until many decades later, that Bataan's and Corregidor's place in the greater war effort slowly began to gain recognition. The U.S. troops serving there, with minimal supplies, outdated weapons, and little food and medicine, held off the enemy for five months in battles that the Japanese High Command expected to take fifty days. Those extra three months enabled the Allies to regroup after Pearl Harbor. Historians, at last, credited the defenders of Bataan and Corregidor with stopping Japanese plans to invade Australia, which became a crucial staging area for allied forces.

Bataan and Corregidor eventually became known as the "Alamo of the Pacific."

CHAPTER 4

Prisoner of the Japanese

Late in the afternoon of May 6, 1942, enemy troops arrived. Tens of thousands of American servicemen and Filipino fighters officially became prisoners of the Japanese.

Their soldiers immediately started to take anything of value from their captives: watches, rings, blankets, and even clothes. Some of the Japanese had watches up to their elbows on both arms.

One of my prized possessions was a scrapbook from my Shanghai days. I hid it on my birthday with very little hope of ever seeing it again.

As hundreds of books have already been written about the horrors of their forty months in captivity, I want to put emphasis in these pages on *why* and *how* John managed to survive that hell. An estimated 42% of the *China Marines* and 37% of the total captured in Asia were not that lucky. (In contrast, the survival rate of American POWs in Germany was 97%.)

The hardships John endured while growing up contributed to his survival. Where life on the farm with all the hard work, few amenities and poor sanitary conditions would once have seemed a tremendous *disadvantage,* as a POW it became a big *asset.* His immune system was much stronger than that of the men who had led a more pampered life. While many

POWs died from dysentery, John never suffered from it. With some luck he survived attacks of malaria, beriberi, dengue fever, and pneumonia.

Weakened from lack of food and fatigue, many prisoners came down with diseases not long after surrender. This was particularly true for those men who had survived the grueling Bataan Death March. Thousands of them died within the first months of captivity.

Shortly after capture the prisoners were assembled at the "92nd garage," a vast, open, cemented area without any protection from the hot sun. They all scrambled to find materials, like old blankets and tarpaper—anything to make a crude shelter. There were no sanitation facilities other than an open pit for human waste.

The Japanese were totally unprepared to feed this huge number of prisoners. It took days before the first meager rations of rice were handed out. As for water, there was just one spigot. Though the men all got turns filling their canteens, it required long hours of standing in line.

During the day we were ordered into work gangs to bury the bodies of Japanese soldiers killed during the invasion. We were not allowed to bury our own dead. I had to watch the bodies of my fallen friends bloat and decay until all that could be seen of them were the big green flies covering the remains.

After almost three weeks at the 92nd garage, the POWs were put aboard ships and taken to Manila. Waiting ashore were Japanese officers on horseback, who formed them into columns and paraded them through the center of Manila, to the old Filipino prison *Bilibid*. This was supposed to be the "parade of shame," showing the Filipinos what had become of the American military. Instead, the Filipinos sympathized with the prisoners and even tried to hand them food.

Bilibid was to become the "repair shop" for prisoners at camps throughout the Philippines who became victims of beatings or accidents. John's friend Bob, unable to work with one leg, spent the entire duration of the war there.

After a short stay in Bilibid, John's unit was sent to Cabanatuan Camp III. They were transported in boxcars— standing room only. The stench became overwhelming during the many hours it took to reach their destination.

On arrival at the new camp John came upon a scene that didn't bode well for the near future. Three army officers, captured after an escape attempt, were tied up at the entrance of the camp. For several days they were mercilessly beaten. Shortly after John arrived the Japanese shot them in the belly, which resulted in a slow, painful death. A firing squad finally gave the *coup de grace.*

A Marine officer asked a Japanese guard who spoke a little English why they didn't just shoot them to begin with. The guard answered, "According to the code of Bushido, death is not a punishment. You have to suffer before you die."

Like most of the men, John had never heard of this "Bushido code," the fighting code of the Japanese warrior. According to that code it was considered cowardice to surrender. Death was the alternative. Anyone who surrendered, in the eyes of the Imperial Forces of Japan, was considered humanity in its lowest form. Any show of pity, sympathy, or compassion was unmanly and violated the Bushido code. Barbaric behavior, such as murder, rape, pillage, and torture was acceptable as long as it was done in the name of the emperor.

We would soon find out what the Bushido code meant to us prisoners. Equally bad was the fact that the Japanese government claimed they never signed the Geneva Convention after WWI, which stood for fair treatment of POWs.

I saw a lot of my buddies being tortured, sometimes for no reason at all. For anything the Japs didn't like about someone they would kick and beat him or execute him by bayonet or beheading. In addition to those tortures and the starvation diet, tropical diseases could kill you. We were constantly surrounded by death, death, and more death.

We used open pit urinals and privies with flies everywhere. Meaningful medical treatment was unavailable. Red Cross packages with supplies, meant for prisoners, were kept by the Japs for their own use.

A routine of desperation was established to take care of the dead and dying. One of the bamboo shacks in the camp was designated as a hospital. Another was to become the "Zero Ward." When a prisoner reached a point where he could no longer take care of basic functions he was moved to the hospital shack and given whatever medical treatment was possible. This was administered with sympathy and encouragement by American medical personnel: captured doctors and corpsmen. Occasionally aspirin was made available. The only—marginally effective—help for POWs with dysentery was burned rice. When a patient's condition got to the point where death was imminent, he was moved to the Zero Ward, meaning there was *zero* chance for survival.

John was part of a group assigned to remove the dead from the Zero Ward. After picking up the bodies they wrapped them in a sheet or blanket. Next they tied that to bamboo poles, which they carried over their shoulders, one man in front and one in the rear. Each day this burial detail checked the body count, which determined the size of grave to be dug. One crew dug a big hole for mass burial, while John's group carried the bodies over a mile-long path towards the grave. They buried between thirty-five and forty corpses daily. After each mass burial a captured chaplain said grace.

The following is taken from John's writings, describing his first months in captivity:

It became immediately apparent that communication with the Japs was a real problem. We could not understand their orders, which were all given in Japanese. Often prisoners were beaten for failing to obey those orders. We quickly learned some of the most common commands. Learning how to count in Japanese became another necessity. We were each assigned a number. During the daily "tenkos" (roll calls) the guards recited the numbers in Japanese. You'd better answer to your number when called!

While at Cabanatuan III, I made a serious assessment of my situation and gave much thought to what I could do to increase my chance of survival. I accepted the fact that I now was at the mercy of barbarians, who considered compassion unmanly and a sign of weakness. The starvation diet of a little rice and whistle weed soup would not sustain a person long. The lack of sanitary facilities could only result in more flies, more diseases, and more deaths. We had absolutely no creature comforts. Besides a lack of food we had no soap, toothpaste or toothbrushes. Any form of recreation to take your mind off your misery was non-existent. My weight didn't help either; rations were the same for everyone, whether you weighed two hundred or one hundred pounds.

So I made my plans carefully. First, I would keep a low profile, blending in with the crowd, thus reducing my chances of random beatings and executions. Then I would get the hell out of Cabanatuan if the opportunity ever presented itself.

John did leave six months later to a place you can only call worse than the one he left. As part of a work detail to clear a jungle for the construction of an airfield he went by boat to the island of Palawan. They arrived in the early evening.

A quick inspection of their new quarters revealed a surprise: *mosquito nets!* Though their "beds" consisted of bamboo slats on a cement floor, like in their previous camp, being protected from mosquito bites was a sure plus point.

As for the food on Palawan, their first meal, consisting of—what else—*rice* elicited some remarks: "Look," one man observed, "We're getting *brown* rice, that's a lot healthier." On closer inspection, the color of the rice came from all the *maggots* crawling around in it. Not knowing where their next meal would be coming from, they ate it anyway, figuring it was a source of protein. The prisoners would eat anything to keep from starving. Monkeys and snakes, if they could catch them, were a welcome addition to their rations.

On Palawan the men first encountered the dreaded "Kempei Tai," the so-called "thought police." They would torture a prisoner if they felt he was having *bad thoughts.* Another reason to keep a low profile!

The Marines of the 4th Regiment stuck together as much as they could. Their motto was: "Surrendered, yes, defeated, no!" Their original proclamation: "Land of the free in forty-three," one year later became: "Home once more in forty-four," and finally: "Home alive in forty-five," before they would be free.

John and his buddies tried to maintain their sense of humor in their misery; they gave their guards funny nicknames and made up silly songs about their lousy food—anything to laugh about. Their watery rice soup was called "lugao." The following song soon made the rounds:

> *Lugao, lugao, eat the stuff you must.*
> *If you eat till satisfied, belly belly bust.*
> *You no eat, then you die, isn't nature grand?*
> *MacArthur come and liberate the bastards of Bataan.*

They would joke, "What is it going to be, the Pearly Gates or the Golden Gate?" John decided to shoot for the Golden Gate. His attitude, no matter the horrors and deprivation, stayed positive. He convinced himself he was going to make it. He never gave up hope; *I wasn't going to let those SOBs bury me!* In spite of the dismal conditions John tried to find something of *beauty* each day: *They couldn't take a glorious sunset away from me.*

Occasionally, the men had some unexpected laughs to help morale:

> *There was a very short, pudgy Jap officer, whose daily morning routine was to show his skills with his samurai sword. We were supposed to watch this spectacle after bowing in the direction of the emperor. This Jap wore tall boots, so we gave him the nickname "Puss n' boots." He would shout and gyrate, lift the sword high above his head and then swing it backward until it almost hit the ground. One time, as he was swinging it backward it hit him right in the fanny. Blood was gushing out. We all cheered and clapped. He never went through that routine again.*

For easier censorship by the Japanese, mail from home was allowed on postcards only. Many of the cards John's mother sent him were returned to her, marked "undeliverable." The cards he did receive usually contained bad news, like the notice of his father's death.

CHAPTER 5

A Life Saving Beating

Luck had a lot to do with John's survival. He defied death at least three times. The first time happened late in 1942, while still at Palawan. I'll let John tell the story:

> *Clearing the jungle included moving huge anthills. These were mounds of earth often ten feet high and twelve feet across, usually filled with snakes, spiders, scorpions, foot-long tropical centipedes, and various other creatures.*
>
> *In early December, while working on such an anthill I suddenly felt a searing pain in my foot. I had been bitten by a centipede. The tropical centipede bite is extremely painful, poisonous, and sometimes fatal. I was dizzy with pain. My buddies carried me down to the American doctor, who regretfully informed me that he had absolutely no medicine for me, not even an aspirin.*
>
> *The pain during the night was unbearable. I remember banging the back of my head against the wall, which felt less painful than my foot. The following morning the doctor told me he had not expected me to live. The pain had decreased a little but my entire leg was swollen and I had a very high fever.*
>
> *The doctor convinced the Japs I was unable to work, so I was allowed to stay in the barracks. Prisoners*

who couldn't work had their already meager rations cut in half.

The next day, while thinking how hungry I was, I noticed a papaya tree near the compound fence with ripe fruit hanging above the fence. Not seeing any guards close by I took a chance and picked one of the papayas. Just as I took my first bite, Sergeant Nichitoni came around the corner and caught me. This Jap was a brutal, sadistic guard, who appeared to enjoy inflicting pain and suffering on American prisoners. He grabbed a piece of steel re-bar and started beating me with it. He beat me from my head to my feet for an extended period of time. I tried to protect my back with my arms. He finally quit, threw the steel down, and walked away.

Both my arms were broken in various places, as well as one shoulder. My entire body ached. For many weeks I urinated blood which, according to the doctor, meant my kidneys had been damaged.

The American doctor made a makeshift splint out of chicken wire, apologizing that it was the best he could do. A few days later John was transferred to Bilibid for further treatment. He never went back to Palawan.

The after effects of that beating plagued John his entire life. When in 1951 he was recommended for commission to become an officer, his repeated kidney shutdowns kept him from passing the required physical exam in the time allotted. In the early '90s the once broken shoulder had to be replaced.

Why would you call this *lucky?* Two years later, when American liberation forces approached Palawan, the Japanese were ordered to kill all remaining prisoners. They were herded into air raid shelters, gasoline was poured in and torches were lit. Except for a few men who managed to escape, they all burned to death. But for the beating, resulting in his transfer, John would have been one of the victims.

John's severe beating had *saved his life.*

CHAPTER 6

No End in Sight

John wished he could have stayed in Bilibid, as food and overall conditions were slightly better than in other camps. However, the Japanese had different plans. As soon as his broken arms were healed he was sent to Cabanatuan Camp I.

Compared to the labor many other POWs were assigned, John's new job was tolerable. He had to work on a "farm," giving him the opportunity once in a while to steal vegetables. His task was to fill a five-gallon bucket with water from a nearby stream, carry it uphill to irrigate the plants, then back down the hill to fill up the bucket again, repeating the process all day long.

Though the job wasn't as bad as previous ones, what made living conditions miserable in this camp were the *bugs:*

> *Inside, the lice and bed bugs ate you up, while outside the mosquitoes and red ants would take their turn. I remember one guy suggesting we bring the ants inside and try to have them eat the bed bugs. Another prisoner standing nearby said, "With our luck the ants would mate with the bed bugs and we'll have something that will both bite and sting."*
>
> *The worst were the flies. They were all around and caused lots of diseases. A fly abatement program sanctioned by the Japanese reduced the death rate*

considerably. The Japs even gave POWs a few cigarettes in exchange for flies.

Talking about cigarettes, there were a few around, either through secret trading with the Filipino villagers or from (rare) packages from home. It's sad to say that some prisoners, desperate for a smoke, traded their meager rice rations for cigarettes. I know with certainty that those men didn't make it back out alive.

During one of his bucket runs John ran into Charlie Kirklen, a skinny redhead from Texas, wearing the remains of a Marine Corps uniform. Though not allowed to talk during working hours, they struck up a quick conversation. Charlie had been at that camp for a while and immediately warned John, "Watch out for 'Air Raid.' He's a sadistic guard who loves to do nothing better than beating us up. When you hear someone yell 'Air Raid,' you know he's close by and you better hide out."

Three years later, during the war trials in Tokyo, "Air Raid," whose real name was Lance Corporal Kazutane Aihara, was sentenced to death by hanging for killing numerous POWs in his charge and participating in the decapitation and stabbing of fifteen other prisoners.

John and Charlie hit it off from the start. Having a "best buddy" in a POW camp, someone who cared for your welfare and helped you stay alive, was of vital importance. The two men continued their conversation in the evening, commiserating about their lack of food, wondering if there was any way to improve that situation. Charlie, a very ingenious individual, came up with an idea: "Johnny, why don't we bake cookies? We could trade them for rice and fruit, and maybe even some medicine." John was skeptical: "Where are you going to find the ingredients, and how are you going to bake them?"

"We'll make an oven from scrap tin," was Charlie's answer. And indeed, with scrap tin he made his oven, primitive at best, but workable.

Now they needed ingredients. The wood chopping detail, which assembled wood for cooking rice, was allowed to get outside the camp to chop down trees. Some of the guards let POWs trade with the Filipinos when no other Japanese were around. Thus, the woodchoppers were able to sneak small quantities of fruit, sugar and rice into the camp.

Charlie worked out a deal with a few of the woodchoppers. Rice for cookies, fruit for cookies, sugar for cookies; it was unbelievable how Charlie could wheel and deal.

Cookie making became our business, with Charlie as the baker. We would soak rice, dry it out, then put it on a board and, with a bottle rolling back and forth, grind it into flour. Next we mixed the flour with sugar and coconut milk. The one vital ingredient still missing was yeast. We found a solution to that problem as well. As aspirin was quite plentiful in this camp, we would feign a headache. We then ground the aspirin the doctor gave us into the batter, as a sub for yeast. As the final ingredient Charlie would mix some limejuice into the batter, and into the oven went the cookies.

The woodchoppers, who had delivered the goods on good faith, were now paid off in cookies. We traded the rest of the batch with whoever had something to eat. And, of course, we ate a lot of them ourselves. I feel that this cookie making deal helped us sustain our health somewhat at Cabanatuan I. For me in particular, this was very important, as I came down with dry beriberi and jaundice during my stay there.

In September of 1943 John and Charlie were both transferred to *Las Piñas,* a prison camp located about seven miles from Manila. A much harder job than at their previous camp was waiting for them: building an airfield. They had to cut down hills and, using narrow gauge railroad equipment, transport the dirt to rice paddies below.

They were working day after day, slowly starving. By now, John had lost at least sixty pounds. As for clothing, they never received anything new while in the tropics. With the intense heat and humidity, in addition to the monsoons, their original clothes had simply rotted away. They worked barefoot, most of them wearing just a G-string, resembling—emaciated—sumo wrestlers. The tropical sun showed no mercy.

In August of '44 a rare delivery of mail and food arrived. We received not only Red Cross packages, which, surprisingly, the Japs actually let us have, but some of us, including me, also got a package from home. Mine was carefully prepared with the help of our family doctor and contained, among others, precious vitamins. Charlie at first didn't want to share in my good fortune: "You need it yourself to stay alive," he said. In the end we enjoyed it together. Combined with the Red Cross package it kept us from starving for several weeks.

It's good we were unaware of our next phase as POWs, a nightmare worse than anything we could have imagined.

CHAPTER 7

Hell Ship to Japan

In September of 1944, John thought liberation was near:

> *An old Navy Chief in our group yelled out to me,*
> *"Boswell, I hear planes and they're not Jap planes." My*
> *response was, "Wishful thinking, Chief." But he was*
> *right. Soon after, Jap planes were falling in flames all*
> *around. American planes began to strafe our area as we*
> *were yelling and screaming to see the Japs being*
> *clobbered. Two Navy planes flew over, wagging their*
> *wings as they passed.*
>
> *We were jubilant; we thought liberation day had*
> *arrived and started thinking about going home, taking a*
> *hot shower, and eating a decent meal.*

Alas, it was not to be. When the Japanese realized
American liberation troops were getting close, they quickly gave
orders to assemble all able-bodied prisoners—men still able to
stand. They were to be transported to Japan to perform slave
labor for the understaffed Japanese factories.

The prisoners were moved to Manila, where they were
loaded aboard ships that were soon dubbed "Hell Ships," for a
journey that defies description.

John's second bit of luck came during the thirty-nine
days of hell on one of those ships, the "Haro Maru." It didn't

take long before the POWs renamed the ship "Horror Maru" or *Benjo* Maru, benjo meaning toilet or s*** in Japanese. The ship was part of a convoy of merchant ships, tankers and escorting naval vessels. As none of the ships had any markings that POWs were aboard, many were sunk by American subs or aircraft.

To give some idea what these ships were like I'll let John do the talking:

Let's go aboard this hell ship, an old rusty Jap freighter. From the dock up a steep gangway. Then down a rope ladder to the forward cargo hold, an area of about 40 x 60 feet. The deck was a mixture of horse droppings from a previous shipment of horses, and coal. Jap officers with swords drawn and enlisted soldiers with rifles with fixed bayonets pushed and shoved POWs against the rear wall, shoulder to shoulder and back against the wall. The second row backed against the chests of the first row. Loading continued in this manner until the hold was jammed with seven hundred POWs. Standing room only. No ventilation, water supply or toilets. When the loading was completed the Jap guards secured all escape routes, leaving only a small area for two people to exit the hold simultaneously.

Four prisoners were assigned at that opening. Their job was to lower four empty five-gallon buckets by rope into the hold for removal of human waste, pulling them up when filled and dumping its contents overboard.

The hold was soon fouled with the stench of human waste. With the tropical heat and no ventilation, life for us became a living hell. It didn't take long before suffocation, starvation, dehydration, and heat exhaustion began to take its toll. Each morning, bodies of the men who had died during the night were hoisted up and tossed into the sea.

As for nourishment, once a day a second bucket was lowered, containing rice balls, the size of a baseball—our only food each day. We were also told to send our canteen up, hopefully to get it filled with water. The canteen became a weapon of life and death. It was life if your canteen happened to be one that got filled and returned to you. Some prisoners went delirious from lack of water, some even tried to kill their fellow men for a sip. Others simply couldn't take it any longer and "willed" themselves to die. They would stare into space and be found dead in the morning.

One day my canteen didn't make it back. I was almost totally dehydrated and wouldn't have lasted through the night if not for my best buddy Charlie, who shared his water with me, not knowing if he would get another ration himself. Without that selfless deed I don't believe I would have survived. It was the second time I escaped death. Charlie remained my best friend until his—too early—death at age sixty-three.

As for a new canteen, I took a replacement from a dead prisoner.

Conditions in the hold worsened as the days progressed. Prisoners with dysentery couldn't wait for the waste bucket. Often, when that bucket, filled to the brim, was hoisted up the rope ladder before being thrown overboard, some of its contents would spill out into the hold. The entire hold resembled one big cesspool.

If that wasn't bad enough, there was the constant worry about being hit by U.S. bombers and submarines, the crews of which had absolutely no clue that American prisoners were aboard. The POWs all knew that, if hit, they didn't have a chance to get out through the one small opening.

One day our convoy did come under attack. With each explosion of torpedoes and depth charges rust particles from the aging ship rained down on us. We had to hold our hands over our mouth and nose to breath. Believers and non-believers alike prayed fervently—

some for survival, others for a direct hit to end their misery.

John's ship was only one of three in his convoy that wasn't torpedoed or bombed.

They didn't make it straight to Japan, though, as planned. Going off-course, zigzagging through the waters to avoid attacks, they wound up in Formosa (now Taiwan) after a stop over in the Hong Kong harbor. After more than five weeks of starvation and dehydration John, like most of the men, couldn't walk down the gangplank; they had to *crawl* down. When a high-ranking Japanese officer came aboard and saw their condition, he immediately ordered food and water. Yes, there were a few compassionate Japanese.

Though John would never have believed it then, Lady Luck had been on his side again; many *hell ships* were torpedoed by American submarines, resulting in the loss of more than five-thousand POWs.

CHAPTER 8

Slave Laborer for Mitsubishi

The nine-week stay in Formosa was a godsend for the POWs; with better food they were able to regain some weight and strength. More medication was made available for the many diseases as well. If they could only have stayed there till the end of the war....

Unfortunately, factories in Japan needed workers badly. In mid-January 1945, the prisoners were loaded aboard the quite modern *Melbourne Maru,* headed for *Moji,* Japan. Conditions on this ship were far better than on the Haro Maru. On January 25 the POWs were put ashore in subzero temperatures.

> *We wore what little was left of our tropical clothing and discarded Japanese uniforms. This gave our battle for survival a whole new dimension. At one point British overcoats were handed out. However, the supply ran out before reaching me.*
>
> *Prior to proceeding north to Sendai the Japs divided us into groups. During the ensuing confusion Charlie and I were separated. I didn't see him again until after the war.*

John's group consisted of about 250 American POWs, some British and a few Dutchmen. The day after arriving in Moji they left the area by train, for an eight-hour trip by narrow gauge rail to the small mining town of *Hosokura*. The further north they traveled the colder it got. Their clothing was woefully inadequate for the bone-chilling weather they were experiencing as they entered the mountains of *Northern Honshu*. On January 28 the prisoners arrived at Sendai Sub-Camp 3B. They were led on foot along a small trail of packed snow to an old, unheated wooden building, which the men soon dubbed the "icebox." This remained John's home for the remainder of the war.

The walls in the barracks consisted of planks with enough space in between for the icy wind to blow straight through. Though each barrack came equipped with two fifty-gallon drums to serve as heaters, the little bit of coal they received was of such inferior quality that it barely threw off any heat. The prisoners soon started to burn what were supposed to be their "pillows," pieces of wood handed to the men on arrival. At night they huddled under their thin, straw-like blankets, trying to share some body heat. John had never been so cold in all his life.

The freezing temperatures, in addition to the starvation diet, took its toll. Men began to die from exhaustion and exposure to the cold. The ground was frozen so hard it was impossible to dig graves for those who died; bodies were stacked in a shack until the spring thaw.

During the day the POWs worked as slave laborers in the Mitsubishi lead and zinc mines. John described the daily routine:

> *Early in the morning, after a miserably cold night in the icebox, we ate a little breakfast, consisting of barley mixed with a bit of rice. Then we were marched to the mine. Here something peculiar happened: we were stopped at the mine entrance and forced to bow to the "Mine God," a statue of crudely carved wood, about a foot tall. The interpreter explained the Mine God as the*

power that held up the mine. He pointed out that the Mine God loved to listen to the human hum or whistle. Whenever he heard those sounds he became so enraptured that he would forget to hold up the mine, resulting in its collapse. Therefore, whistling or humming was strictly forbidden.

We tried our best to sabotage the work in the mines, delaying the procedures. Sometimes we were able to put rocks on the rail of the mine carts, making them flip over. Other times, during blasting, we quickly blew out our lamps, pretending the blast was to blame.

All morning long we worked in the mine, then ate the little food provided for us at noon, and back to work through the afternoon and early evening. Before going back to our barracks, we were assembled again at the mine entrance, forced to face the Mine God, and bow again as a way of expressing our thanks for holding up the mine for us.

At one point I thought the routine at the mine entrance was so ridiculous, that I failed to bow. I immediately was hit with a rifle butt in my neck. I decided from then on to go along with this farce, as it wasn't worth getting beaten up for.

Although taken to and from the camp to the mine by Japanese guards, inside the mines the POWs were supervised by civilian "honchos," who were not quite as brutal as their military counterparts.

In February of '45, one month after arrival, John contracted pneumonia.

Two weeks of my life became a complete blank. The last thing I remember before I blacked out was severe chest pains with each breath I took. When I woke up I found myself in a small isolated room with other sick prisoners. Two American army doctors were in charge. I recall trying to stand up and falling on the cement floor, injuring my knees and elbows. One of the doctors, a colonel, helped me back to my blanket, cleaned my wounds, and said how lucky I had been that the Japanese had decided to release some Red Cross medical supplies, including penicillin. He then told me that I had been in a coma for fourteen days and that they had not expected me to live.

I had defied death for the third time!

The camp director, whose main task was filling the daily quota for mine workers, cared little about John's welfare. Though under strict orders from his doctor to rest in order to get his strength back, John was forced to return to work just a few days after coming out of the coma. Too weak to walk the mile-long trail to the mines, other prisoners had to carry him to and from work, where he was assigned a "sitting" job, breaking up large chunks of carbide into small pieces, to be used for light in the miners' hats.

John slowly regained enough strength to return to his regular job as a *mucker*, shoveling zinc and lead ore into mine carts after blasting. It was now back to the old routine; working in the mine during the day and freezing in the *icebox* at night, while slowly starving on an inadequate diet of a barley mixture.

During his illness a talented POW made John's canteen into a piece of art. He sharpened an army knife and engraved John's name in decorative script, as well as the names of all the prison camps John had survived. The artist died before it was completely finished. The canteen became the one and only memento John brought home from his time as a POW.

Day after miserable day slowly passed as we struggled to survive. Spring finally arrived. We began to thaw out—life became a little less miserable. At the end of March all of us received a large Red Cross package with food and clothing—a most welcome gift!

In August of '45, shortly after the dropping of the second atom bomb, a Red Cross representative entered the camp, giving the prisoners the news they had long been waiting for: Japan had surrendered. THE WAR WAS OVER!

Work in the mines suddenly ceased. Japanese guards left in a hurry, leaving their rifles behind. One camp commandant stayed on. Fearing retributions for the deplorable conditions of the men he shouted, "You have to gain weight, you have to gain weight."

After suffering unimaginable hardships for forty months John was a free man again. He had made it—he had survived! Surrender had come in the nick of time. Official orders found after the war concerning the nearly 100,000 allied prisoners of the Japanese who were still alive in July of 1945 stated: "Whether they are destroyed individually or in groups, or however it is done, with mass bombing, poisonous smoke, poisons, drowning, decapitation, or whatever else, dispose of the prisoners as the situation dictates. In any case it is the aim not to allow the escape of a single one, to annihilate them all, and not leave any traces." Documents found regarding John's camp indicated that all POWs were scheduled to be executed on August 28.

The newly liberated men were informed to remain in the camp until further instructions arrived. B-29s flew over and dropped food and clothing, packed in huge oil drums. Very sadly, some of the drums broke loose from their parachutes, killing three Americans. What a way to die after having survived for so long!

The order to move out finally reached us. We were taken by train to Sendai for delousing, processing and rehabilitation. It's hard to describe, after forty months of living in filth and deprivation, how it felt taking that first hot shower, eating a real meal and slipping into clean clothes. To my regret I was declared unfit for flying home—too many open sores and overall weakness. I had lost half of my normal weight: from 220 to 110 pounds. I became a bed patient on the hospital ship Rescue and settled in for good food, good rest, and good people, who really cared about my welfare. I was finally GOING HOME!

*John's decorated canteen cup—
the only reminder of his battle for survival*

CHAPTER 9

Post-War Years in the Marine Corps

After returning to the U.S. John spent the next six months in the Pensacola Naval Hospital. As this was only ninety miles from his home, his mother and brothers often visited him.

During one of those visits his mom brought him a package that had arrived from Australia in 1943. John couldn't believe his eyes—it was his *scrapbook from Shanghai,* completely intact. He never did understand how in the world that book could have survived, who had found it on Corregidor, and how it went from the Philippines to Australia. Knowing where to send it hadn't been hard; there were enough letters from his mother with a return address.

The doctors in the hospital healed his *body* as much as possible but the term "post traumatic stress disorder" had not yet been invented. John was on his own. The last comment the doctor made to him before being discharged was, "Congratulations, Boswell, for making it back, but don't expect to live beyond fifty." John decided to ignore those words; he proved the doctor wrong by thirty-three years.

When anyone after the war asked him about his experiences, John was evasive and clammed up. He told me many years later, "People would never have believed me if I'd told them what it was really like."

In April '46, after his discharge from the hospital and upon returning to Bonifay, John's mother invited friends and family over to greet him. One elderly lady said to him, "You know, Ray, you were so lucky not to be in the States during these war years; we had all this rationing and shortages." That proclamation proved John right—people had no idea what he had endured.

For the next thirty years John hardly ever said a word about his prison camp years, seemingly trying to erase them from his mind.

During his leave in Bonifay, John enjoyed his mother's southern cooking, became re-acquainted with old friends and relatives and…started dating again. John explained to me later how the POWs, slowly starving to death, had zero interest in talking or thinking about girls and sex. All they could think about was *food*, how to scrounge enough up to stay alive.

Upon discharge from the Navy Hospital John's CO approached him about re-enlistment: "Go home for a while, take all the time you want, and then decide what you want to do. When you're ready let me know."

It didn't take long for John to make up his mind. He now had nine years in the service, almost half-way towards a twenty-year career and retirement. He signed up for another five years in April of 1946. With no promotions for enlisted men during his imprisonment, he climbed three ranks in rapid succession and became a tech sergeant.

His first post-war assignment was on an exhibition ship, traveling from harbor to harbor, showing what jungle warfare had been like and occasionally re-creating invasions. The crew, part Navy and part Marine Corps, officers as well as NCOs, were all combat veterans. John with his deep, melodious voice soon became the radio announcer. The crew was wined and dined wherever they went. In John's own words:

Bar Harbor topped all other ports; they really rolled out the red carpet for us. Tables were piled high with Maine lobster and a variety of food fit for a king. In the evening they organized a formal dance with lovely girls in beautiful evening gowns. We Marines, in Dress Blues, enjoyed an unforgettable evening.

John served about one year on that ship. To his great regret the exhibition ships were discontinued towards the end of 1947. His next assignment was of a more sober nature: Escort duty. He was to bring bodies of Marines killed overseas back to the nearest of kin. Sometimes the recipients were grateful to have their loved-ones back for a decent burial; other times people in their grief expressed bitterness: "Why did you come back and my son did not?"

In the fall of 1948, John's Commanding Officer asked if he was interested in *embassy duty*. John, always ready for new adventure, found it intriguing. He signed up.

This was a totally new concept, a new "mission." Marine Security Guards (MSGs) were assigned at U.S. embassies in foreign countries to prevent classified material from falling into the wrong hands. Marines had to provide protection twenty-four hours a day, 365 days a year. Qualifications were stringent: the men had to be single, second generation Americans, of above average intelligence, and cleared by the FBI. The first embassies to be manned with MSGs were mostly in Europe, less than ten in total. A few weeks of instructions followed John's election to MSG.

In December John found himself anxiously waiting, as one of the "chosen few" to hear his assignment—in what exciting or exotic city he was going to spend his next two or more years. "Stockholm, Sweden, Master Sergeant Bert Jakobson," the announcement came. Then, "Lisbon, Portugal, Tech Sergeant John Boswell." John was to be the NCO in charge of five lower-ranked men.

As the Portuguese government refused to let MSGs wear uniforms John received an extra allowance to go shopping for civilian clothes: suits, white shirts and ties.

John arrived in Lisbon early in February of 1949. His first task was to set up the entire administration, assigning duties to the Marines in his charge and making sure the mission became successful. The two-week training proved to be totally inadequate; he had to use his ingenuity and common sense to get the security work rolling. Their main task was to make routine checks of embassy offices. Diplomats, not used to any security before, were at first resentful when given violation slips for leaving classified information out or in an unsecured location. Eventually they resigned to the close control and started to appreciate the work the Marines did.

A whole new life started for John, different from anything he had experienced before. As the NCO in charge, he was invited to many of the parties of the diplomatic corps. John, the farm boy, was now hobnobbing with high-ranking diplomats. Yet he also befriended Portuguese civilians working for the embassy, like chauffeurs and mailroom clerks. They showed him where to buy the best wines and gave him a glimpse of life in Portugal few outsiders experience.

At an art exhibit, sponsored by the British Cultural Center, he met Siegfried Hahn, a South African artist, famed for his watercolors and oil paintings that depicted scenes in and around Lisbon. It was the start of a life-long friendship.

One day Siegfried invited John to the unveiling of a portrait he had made. "Where are we going?" John asked. "I'll tell you in a while," came the answer. They traveled thirty minutes by train to *Cascais,* known as the village of "fishermen and kings." After a short taxi ride they arrived at a huge mansion. That's when Siegfried spoke up: "John, you are about to meet royalty." King Umberto, the deposed king of Italy, had commissioned the artist to paint his portrait.

Soon John was introduced and shook hands with King Umberto. "What do you think of my portrait?" the king asked him after the unveiling. John, trying to act nonchalant, as if he were in the habit of giving art critique, answered that he found the likeness extraordinary. The three chatted for a while and had a drink. John told me it was an experience he wouldn't soon forget.

During the spring of 1950, Siegfried, an excellent tennis player, taught John how to play the game. John quickly caught on and truly enjoyed the sport. They played almost every Saturday. During one of their games John kept looking at an adjacent court, where two young women were hitting the ball. "I know one of the girls," Siegfried said when he noticed John's interest, "Let's invite them for a drink after the game."

The rest, as the saying goes, is history.

Formal picture taken to send to his mother
before leaving for Portugal—January '49

CHAPTER 10

Paula Growing Up

When John was not quite five years old, over 4600 miles away in Rotterdam, The Netherlands, I was introduced into the world. I was the second child and had a brother Loek (pronounced Luke), who was three years older.

When I was a toddler, my parents bought a house in Scheveningen bordering on the North Sea, a side arm of the Atlantic Ocean. It was part seaside resort and part fisherman's village, a suburb of The Hague.

Our street, the "Zeeweg" (*Sea Way* in translation), was on an incline, leading up to the "Boulevard," the avenue parallel to the sea, lined with outdoor cafés, fancy shops and souvenir stands. Wide, beautiful beaches were just a few minutes away.

We kids *loved* the Zeeweg, where there was always something to do. We played with tops, marbles, hoops, jumped rope or, on rainy days, assembled in the house of our neighbors across the street. They had two daughters, Nora and Meta, one and two years older than me. Luke and I spent a lot of time with them. The third floor of their house was a huge attic, literally loaded with toys and games.

During the summer the four of us spent all day long at the beach, a two-minute walk from our home. There was a fenced-in beach area with lifeguards, called the "Volksbad," *People's Bath.* For very little money you could buy a summer-long pass. We started swimming in the North Sea when the water climbed to around 60 degrees. The few times it hit 70 we were in heaven.

My parents were quite well off financially. Loek and I wore expensive clothes and we had a live-in maid. My father was one of the first to own a car.

Our peaceful and prosperous existence came to an abrupt halt in the early '30s with the arrival of *The Great Depression.* Around 1932 my dad's flourishing business went *kaput.* With it went the life we had been used to. No more maid. When we outgrew our store-bought clothes, my grandmother, "Oma" in Dutch, came to the rescue. An accomplished seamstress, she would sew clothes for us, usually with material she bought as remnants at a flea market. For winter coats she took my parents' old coats apart and turned the material inside out to make us new ones. Dresses getting too short? No problem. I remember one red polka-dotted dress that got too short. Each year she would add four inches of solid red material to the bottom until I finally burst out of it.

At the beginning of one summer Loek and I discovered we had both outgrown last year's bathing suits. (Boys didn't wear trunks yet.) There was no money for new suits, so my mother decided to *knit* us new suits from some left-over yarn. Though the sweaters she knit for us were lovely, a hand-knit bathing suit didn't exactly represent the height of fashion to a nine-year old girl. For a twelve-year old boy it was downright embarrassing. However, as obedient kids, we kept our mouths shut and wore the darn things.

If we wanted something new, like a bike, we had to wait for our birthday, and it sure was *not* a brand-new one. For treats on special occasions we would get pastries at a day-old bakery. Frankly, they were yummy! I had two favorites: chocolate covered creampuffs with whipping cream inside, and a three inch high meringue torte filled with chocolate fudge. Yes, my love for anything chocolate started early.

No matter how little money we had, we never failed to celebrate "Sinterklaas" (short for Sint Nikolaas—Dutch for

Saint Nicholas) on December 5. Early Dutch settlers in the States made this into Santa Claus and it became associated with Christmas.

It's impossible to describe to a non-Dutchman what Sinterklaas is all about. Besides buying presents we all spent hours, sometimes days, making gag gifts for other members of the family. Each present had to be accompanied by a funny poem directed at the receiver, which had to be read out loud. It was an evening we looked forward to for months. Even we kids, saving up our pennies, bought presents for everyone in the family.

It was amazing what my mother could do with little money. We never felt we were poor or deprived. And what remained constant while growing up was the fact my mom was *always* waiting for us when we got home from school, something few children experienced many decades later.

My father had started to work as a salesman in butcher shop machinery—on commission only. Some Saturdays he would come home without a paycheck. Other times he would say, "Well, I didn't get any money, but look at the steaks one of my customers gave me!" A scrumptious meal soon graced our dining table. What a treat! After dinner Pop confessed that it was meat from the "horse butcher." Honestly, it didn't taste bad at all and was definitely better than some of our *meatless* dinners. Though we loved the *all pancake* meals, we were less enchanted when we had to eat "grutjes" (grits?) for dinner, a kind of cream of wheat cooked in buttermilk and served with syrup on top.

Though my parents couldn't really afford it, they insisted I take piano lessons when I was about ten years old. "It's a social skill that will be a great asset as you grow older," they reasoned. I was less enthusiastic and hated the daily practicing. I suffered through scales and etudes for five agonizing years before they accepted the fact I had absolutely no talent.

In the first four grades of elementary school there was no homework. I made good grades, usually eights and nines (ten being an absolute perfect score). However, as soon as we started to get homework my grades dropped dramatically. I don't know why, but I simply refused to do homework. At the end of sixth grade I had to take an entrance exam to be accepted into a college-prep high school. I just squeaked by. The only subjects in high school I enjoyed were foreign languages: English, French and German.

I haven't mentioned yet that in 1929 and 1931 two siblings were born: Hans and Toto, five and seven years younger than me. Because of the age difference, I didn't spend much time with them. On the other hand, I spent a lot of my spare time with Loek. He was very intelligent—a brilliant student. Together we managed a stamp collection, and worked on all sorts of puzzles and brain teasers. We even issued our own—very primitive—puzzle *magazine* with self-invented puzzles. Occasionally we submitted our puzzles to the "Denksport"—*Think Sport* in translation—a nationwide puzzle publication. A few times our inventions were actually accepted. Seeing our puzzles printed up in the *Denksport* with the mention: *submitted by Mr. L. (or Miss P.) van Dalsum* was a huge thrill. I'm sure the editors had no idea we were just kids. We didn't receive any money for this—it was just the honor.

Once Loek and I wanted to see a historic film about the life of Dutch Prince William of Orange. To raise the necessary fifty cents for admission we decided to hold a *yard sale*. Mom contributed some of her kitchen stuff and we dug into our old toys. Soon we were ready to set up shop in our front yard. By the evening we had enough to pay for the tickets. Proud about our accomplishments we entered the theater a few days later. In history class we had learned the story, so we knew that at the end Prince William was killed. About an hour into the movie we knew the end was near. We got fidgety at first, then more apprehensive about what was to happen and finally we got so scared to see the actual murder scene that we ran out of the theater before the end. *All that work for nothing!*

When Shirley Temple mania hit Holland I became a big fan. I begged my parents for the 25 cents it cost to see a matinee. I could sing all the songs from every movie. In school they often asked me to sing and act out "On the good ship Lollipop"— my first encounter with the English language!

Loek graduated from high school in '38. There was, of course, no money for college. Scholarships didn't exist and besides, he was needed to contribute to our meager income. He became an apprentice in an accountant's firm and immediately started to take classes to advance. When Mom was able to find a part-time job as secretary for an attorney, our financial situation became a little rosier.

In the late 1930s we heard a lot of scary news about Hitler and the Nazi party. For a while many Dutchmen stayed optimistic: "Holland remained neutral during WWI, why would they now invade our little country; what use could we be to Hitler?"

People visiting the big cities in Germany came back with different views. "Hitler is crazy. He's not going to be satisfied until all of Europe belongs to him." Young German children were indoctrinated into the "Hitler Youth," often against their parents' wishes. Young, blue-eyed, blonde women were encouraged and given awards for becoming mothers for the "Reich," to produce perfect specimens.

If the scare of a possible invasion of Hitler's armies wasn't enough, a devastating polio epidemic spread through Europe. "Stay away from crowds, don't gather in stores," read the headlines. There was no vaccine—Dr. Salk was still an unknown. The threat of becoming disabled for life was dreadful. Everyone was advised to get out of the cities.

In complete panic over the safety of her children, my mom came up with a brilliant idea. As we lived in a resort town it was easy to rent out the whole house to vacationers during the month of August. With that extra income Mom and her three youngest, along with her sister Loes, went to "Monschau," an adorable village just across the German border. Pop and Loek, unable to take time off from their jobs, stayed with relatives.

It was general knowledge that at the Dutch/German border, cheap German marks were available. While the rate of exchange at official banks was one guilder to one mark, at the border you could get three marks for every guilder. *To this day I have no idea how and why this worked.* Everyone had heard of it, and lots of people took advantage of it. With triple the rent we received for our house we spent a wonderful month-long vacation, and all three of us kids were outfitted with new clothes and shoes for the coming winter. Best of all, after we returned home the polio scare had greatly diminished.

As our vacation had been so successful and inexpensive, my mother decided to do it again in '39. We chose a different town. As before, I had to entertain the younger kids while Loes and Mom lazed around and had "Kaffee mit Kuchen" (coffee and pastries) each afternoon. Having just finished my second year of high school German, I figured I could combine that baby-sitting chore with improving my fluency in the language. So instead of the suggested hike up the hills I schlepped the kids with me to stores in town. I always asked for an item I knew they weren't selling, which would get a conversation going. My German improved greatly.

With all the sensational newspaper articles and radio broadcasts during the last few months about an impending war, my father had been against our going to Germany from the moment my mother had started to plan this four-week trip. Now, just a few weeks into our vacation he wrote: *In view of the threatening and dangerous circumstances I urgently advise you to come home at once. If you wait much longer you may not be able to find a train home.*

Almost seventy years later I found that letter, together with several others my dad wrote, in a folder with old family pictures.

My mom was having a wonderful time and didn't want to leave early; she didn't think a few weeks would make a difference. Besides, since we had rented out our house in Scheveningen, there was no place to go home to.

Not long after, the decision was taken out of our hands; *Hitler invaded Poland.*

The Dutch Government ordered all vacationers in Germany to come home at once. We hurriedly packed our suitcases and set out for the railroad station, hoping to catch a train shortly. Instead, we found throngs of people already waiting to find a train—any train heading west, in the general direction of Holland. All we could do was join the crowd.

Three trains and endless hours later we at long last reached the Dutch border. By then it was midnight—no more trains until early the following morning. We slept on wooden benches in the station's waiting room. The next day we finally made it home. The entire trip had taken us almost thirty hours, more than ten times the normal schedule.

Months full of anxiety followed our return. What was going to happen to our little country? Was Holland going to be Hitler's next victim?

Loek, Paula, Hans and Toto on the beach

Loek and Paula in knit bathing suits

School picture of Paula and Hans—
eleven and six years old in hand-knit sweaters

The house of the van Dalsum family on the Zeeweg

CHAPTER 11

Holland under Nazi Regime

After the invasion of Poland most everybody in Holland had somber thoughts about the future. Though a few optimistic souls were positive Hitler would leave our country alone, the majority of the Dutch felt sure we would be next.

For years my mother had enjoyed listening to German music stations on the radio. She loved Franz Lehár operettas and the melodious voice of famous tenor Richard Tauber. Now suddenly, each time we tuned into a German station all we heard was Hitler's screaming, penetrating voice, and his adoring countrymen shouting in unison, *Sieg heil, Sieg heil*—hail to victory.

It came as a comfort to hear our country didn't stand alone—we had allies! As soon as Hitler marched into Poland, England and France declared war on Germany. (Russia became Hitler's foe as well a year later.)

My parents, like many Dutchmen, started to hoard food, to "hamster," as it's called in Dutch. "Are you hamstering yet?" was the topic of many conversations. As imports would become scarce first, we stocked up on coffee beans, tea leaves, and cocoa.

The first three months of 1940 elapsed with little change. "Was it possible?" some started to wonder, "Had Hitler changed his plans? Was Holland going to remain neutral like in WWI?"

The answer came soon enough: On April 9 Hitler's troops invaded Denmark and Norway. That's when we knew with certainty Holland was doomed—it was only a matter of time. In spite of reassurances from the Dutch Prime Minister: "Holland's neutrality is not going to be violated," Hitler's armies invaded not only Holland, but Belgium, Luxemburg, and France as well in the early morning hours of May 10, 1940.

The majority of the Dutch population had always been fiercely patriotic. They loved their Royal Family, the *House of Orange.* Shortly after the news about the invasion spread, many Dutchmen, old and young alike, started marching through the streets, proclaiming their loyalty to the queen by waving Dutch flags and wearing red, white, blue, and orange clothes. Others, demonstrating their enthusiasm while they could, grabbed each other by the arm, singing loudly, "Oranje boven, oranje boven, leve the koningin. (Orange above all, long live the queen.)

Early in the afternoon the Dutch police, on orders from our government, started to arrest all Germans living in Holland, for fear they may be spies. Some protested, saying they were Dutch citizens. There was a simple test to determine whether someone was of German descent. The letter "g" and the combination "ch" in the Dutch language both have a harsh, guttural sound, almost impossible to pronounce for a foreigner. So, if in doubt about people's nationality the police demanded: "Say *Scheveningen.*" Some tried: "Uh, *Shayfaningen?*" Off to jail they went, though their imprisonment didn't last long.

The Dutch Marines, Holland's toughest fighting force, fought tenaciously. This greatly annoyed Hitler, who had expected his armies to just march in. After four days of opposition, he gave Queen Wilhelmina an ultimatum: "Either you surrender unconditionally or I'll bomb all your cities flat."

On May 14, 1940 the queen surrendered and fled to England, from where she hoped to guide the country. Her daughter, Princess Juliana, went to Canada with her children.

Juliana's husband, Prince Bernhard, stayed with Queen Wilhelmina in London and joined the British RAF.

Regrettably, Hitler's threat was not an idle one. A large squadron of bombers was already on its way to Rotterdam. They received the surrender message too late and bombed the entire heart out of that city. Numerous lives were lost. It took many years after the war to rebuild. Our family also lost a valuable possession in that bombardment: my father's solid gold pocket watch, which he had pawned for some much needed cash a few months earlier. The pawnshop was destroyed.

Half a century later, whenever I talked about my experiences during WWII someone invariably would ask in all seriousness, "Why didn't your family flee to England?"

I couldn't help chuckle at that naïve question. How did they expect us to get there? In a rowboat, crossing the one hundred mile wide, mine-infested North Sea? And what would have happened after arriving in England? Would a British family enthusiastically have welcomed six strangers with no money? Sure, a few well-to-do individuals with connections were able to charter a plane to get out before the surrender. I also know of several young men who managed to sneak through heavily armed borders to reach Switzerland. But for my family, as was the case with 99% of the population, there was no way out. We were stuck and had to learn to live with our fate.

Holland was now an occupied country. We were completely under Nazi control. Germans and pro-German Dutchmen, whom we considered traitors, replaced most Dutch personnel in leading government positions. Newspapers abruptly stopped printing international news. All you read about was Hitler's advances and successes.

Soon German tanks started to roll into town. Everywhere you looked you saw Nazi uniforms and heard German spoken.

We observed a peculiar sight shortly after German soldiers marched in: they made a beeline to stores selling *butter*, which they proceeded to eat right out of the package. Obviously they had been on very low-fat rations for a while.

What did the occupation mean to me—a fifteen year old? Not so much at first. I still went to school, played hockey, and tennis. We were free to go anywhere on our bikes, while public transportation stayed intact.

The financial situation became worse for my family. The company my father was working for as a salesman imported its wares from *Germany*. That of course stopped abruptly with the onset of the war. All German factories had to switch production to aid the war effort. In other words, Pop was out of a job. To make ends meet, he cashed in his small life insurance policy and found a salesman's job—commission only—selling Dutch merchandise.

Gradually new rules and regulations were implemented. A curfew was established, which meant nobody could be outside after 10:00 p.m. All Dutchmen had to wear an ID tag around their neck. Cars were confiscated for high-ranking German officers. Whenever, in the midst of a Dutch radio broadcast, we suddenly heard: *Achtung, Achtung* (attention) we knew new restrictions were going into effect or we had to hand in some of our possessions needed by the Germans. One day Dutch citizens were ordered to hand in all decorative objects made out of metal, like brass candelabras, copper planters, etc. which were sent to factories to be melted and made into weapons and ammunition. We didn't always fully comply. For all I know, some of our valuables may still be buried in our backyard in Scheveningen.

Fearing we would be listening to the BBC—and find out what was really happening—the High German Command demanded the surrender of all broadband radios. We complied by handing in our big radio but kept a little one, well hidden of course. The Nazis did allow us to listen to a simple, government controlled radio with only a few stations, airing propaganda for the "Reich" and militant German songs. Talking about songs, it became a crime to sing or play the Dutch national anthem.

By early 1941 food and textiles were no longer available without a ration card. Imported supplies, like tea, coffee, and spices became impossible to get except on the black market at outrageous prices. But, we still were not *suffering*; we had a house with gas, electricity, and hot water.

The people who really began to feel the oppression were the Jews. Many German Jews, like Anne Frank's family had fled to Holland when Hitler, with his anti-Semitic policies, came to power. Already early in 1941 all Jews had to wear the yellow star of David. NO JEWS ALLOWED became a familiar sign on public places like parks and beaches. Later in 1941 their situation worsened; no Jew was safe anymore. The dreaded Gestapo, an acronym for Geheime Staats Polizei—secret state police—held *razzias (*raids), picking up Jews and sending them, as we later heard, to concentration camps. Many, for fear of their life, went in hiding.

At my high school I had several Jewish classmates. One day, on entering my classroom after a long weekend there were quite a few empty desks. My friends and I looked at each other in horror: "Where's Bob, and Annie, and Lientje?" We had no clue what happened—either they had gone in hiding or they were picked up by the Gestapo. We wouldn't find out about their fate until after the war.

One of my mother's best friends was Jewish. Her Christian husband came to our house one morning with the sad news she had to go in hiding; *onderduiken* it's called in Dutch, *to dive under* in translation.

Four years later we heard what happened to her. She had been living with a Dutch family in a secluded place until early 1945. Because of her distinct facial features it was very dangerous for her to venture outside. Slowly the continued confinement started to depress her to the point that she proclaimed one day she simply had to get some fresh air. "I'll only be gone for ten minutes," she told her hostess. She never returned. Her husband later heard she was gassed in one of the concentration camps.

Goodhearted people who hid Jews in their homes were in just as great a danger of their lives as the Jews themselves. Often during razzias the host family was shot on the spot.

It was distressing to see how some Dutchmen became traitors. For a monetary reward they turned whole Jewish families in to the Gestapo. Many such traitors joined a pro-Nazi organization, the NSB (a national socialist movement), for the benefits membership brought: better housing, jobs, and extra food rations.

On the lighter side, after I turned seventeen, my parents allowed me to take dancing lessons: ballroom dancing. We learned to dance to music from "Victor Sylvester," sort of boring, very *un-jazzy* dance music. At the culmination of the course a formal "ball" was organized. Because of the (newly established) 8:00 p.m. curfew, it started at five o'clock. As a long evening gown—which I didn't own—was required, my mom dug up something quite ugly from an old trunk. My date, another participant at the dance school, picked me up at 4:30, *on his bicycle,* which he left at my house. We proceeded to walk, in our evening clothes, to a streetcar, which transported us to the ballroom.

Over sixty years later I thought of that escapade when I witnessed how one of my granddaughters attended her senior ball. Wearing a high-fashioned evening gown, with her boyfriend in a fancy tuxedo, they were whisked away in a limo. The contrast could not have been greater.

In the fall of 1942 bad news arrived for my family; anyone living within a short distance from the beach had to evacuate. Hitler's plans were not only to erect an "Atlantic defense wall" to keep the enemy out, but also to build bases from which to shoot V-2s, a long-range missile, to England. In other words, we had to leave our house, take all our belongings, and move. Now came the crucial question: "Where to?"

After much searching we found to our dismay that there was literally nothing available in The Hague for a family of six. The only suitable place we could find was a "war-built" apartment (which meant no luxuries like elevators) in Rotterdam, about fifteen miles away. As an added nuisance we heard that new phone lines were impossible to get.

Not knowing if we would ever see our home in Scheveningen again, my father sold it to a speculator. The cash we received for that house proved a godsend to us; very carefully handled, it lasted till almost the end of the war. Three years later we discovered that the house survived but that the buyer died in a German concentration camp.

I despised moving to Rotterdam. I hated to leave all my friends, clubs, and everything else familiar behind. I wasn't thrilled about my new high school either and often played hookie together with another rebellious girl. One time we brazenly took the train to The Hague to go shopping during school hours. I wrote the notes, explaining my absences, myself. Once, when I really was sick and my mother wrote a note, the school contacted her to ask if it was legit, as the writing looked different from other notes. My mother, having no idea what her seemingly obedient daughter had been up to, was indignant. "Of course I wrote that note myself," she wrote back.

As for our new living quarters, my parents had chosen the top (fourth) floor, as it had two much needed extra bedrooms in the attic. We did a lot of stair climbing over the next eighteen months. I remember having a slightly overweight boyfriend for a short while. Whenever he picked me up at our apartment, he would just stand there huffing and puffing after I opened the door.

Our main rooms had several large windows, which made it difficult for us to comply with the Nazi's very strict black-out rules. Windows had to be completely darkened, so not an iota of light could be seen from the sky by enemy planes. If curtains didn't cover the windows fully, you had to put strips of black paper over the exposed spots.

We heard the droning of British bombers flying over Rotterdam almost nightly. Whenever air raid alarms blared, we had to get up and ready ourselves to leave the house in case of a bombardment. Not until the *all clear* sounded could we go back to bed.

Once, early in the evening, the alarms stayed on for a long time. Wondering what was happening, we cautiously stepped out onto our balcony to have a look. We were in shock! In the distance we saw flames shooting up high into the sky, spreading out over a large area near the harbor. The next morning we heard that bombs, meant for German war ships lying in the harbor, had mistakenly wiped out an entire neighborhood. Many civilians lost their lives, and hundreds were wounded. It was the worst bombing of Rotterdam since the beginning of the war.

The only enjoyable activity I found in Rotterdam's high school was a drama club. I often got *starring* roles. One early evening, after rehearsals, I rode home on my old bicycle. To call my bike *old* is an understatement; it was, by then, a piece of junk. While going down an incline, the main part of the bike just collapsed. I more or less flew through the air and slammed with my chin against the cobblestones. There was blood all over. A Good Samaritan helped me to get home. It was now almost 8:00 p.m.—curfew was starting.

Looking at the deep, bleeding gash in my chin, my parents knew they had to find a doctor immediately. Holding a small towel against my wound, my mom and I set out on a fifteen-minute walk to the nearest doctor's house. Knowing the consequence of being seen by soldiers after curfew we stayed close to the buildings, ducking in and out of portals. At each corner we looked around carefully and, if no soldiers were in sight, dashed across. "Stop or I'll shoot," we suddenly heard. My heart was pounding. What were we going to do? Mom, waving her arms, bravely walked over to the soldier and explained why we were out. Though he understood and told us we could continue on, two blocks later we were stopped again.

This time the German soldier examined our ID papers with great scrutiny and made an elaborate report on the reason why we were on the street after curfew.

Being stopped by enemy soldiers was only one of my concerns. All the while I was thinking, what am I going to look like, will my face be marred forever?

We finally reached the doctor who cleaned the wound and put in stitches." Is it going to leave a scar?" I asked him anxiously. "Don't worry," he reassured me "You were lucky the wound was on the inside of your chin; no one will know the difference." What a relief! I thanked him profusely.

After receiving new threats and orders to get off the street during our return trip, we made it home at last. We were both thrilled that my mishap would not leave any permanent traces.

A much worse accident happened a month later.

CHAPTER 12

Tragedy Strikes

As new jobs were extremely hard to find, my brother Loek continued working at an accountant's office in The Hague, commuting daily by train. He usually returned home by 7:00 p.m.

I will never forget January 14, 1943. We were waiting with dinner. No sign of Loek at the expected hour. At 8:00 we all started to get worried. By nine o'clock we didn't know what to think anymore. Dinner remained unserved. None of us wanted to go to bed. We happened to have a houseguest, an old friend of my mother's who tried to cheer us up. She recited a Dutch poem, which in translation more or less says: "A person often suffers the most by the suffering he *fears* but which may never come. That way he suffers more than God intended." We all prayed our worries would soon prove groundless.

For what seemed endless hours not a word was spoken; we were all occupied with our own thoughts, hoping fervently for a simple explanation.

Suddenly, at about 10:30, the shrill sound of the intercom made us jump. It was a policeman at the main entrance, asking for the head of the house to meet him downstairs. A *policeman*...that sounded ominous. Our hopes evaporated.

My fifty-four year old father walked down the four flights of stairs. Fifteen minutes later he came back, ashen-faced. He managed to utter the words, "It's terrible, terrible."

My brother Loek, at age twenty-one, was dead. He had somehow fallen between the railroad platform and the arriving train and was crushed to death. As we had no phone it took four hours to relay the message.

We were all sobbing uncontrollably, stunned, in total disbelief. This couldn't happen to our family. We started to lay blame for the cause of the accident: the crowd on the platform for having pushed him, the war for the shortage of trains, anything to keep from going crazy.

My father decided to go to the hospital in The Hague to bid a final goodbye to his son. With the *after curfew permit* the policeman had given him he was able to take a late-night train. On arriving at the hospital, my dad heard Loek had still been alive and conscious for several hours. His face was not injured but his pelvic bones were crushed and there was much internal bleeding. Other than administer pain medications there was nothing the doctors could have done. My mother did not go to the hospital—she preferred to remember her oldest child the way she had seen him last.

The accident was front-page news the following evening, including name and address. Not long after the newspaper was delivered, a lady arrived at our door, asking to speak to my parents. "Tell her to go away, I don't want to see anybody," my grieving mother said. When I relayed those words to our visitor she told me, "I thought they may want to know how it happened; I was with him." I invited her in. Soon we heard all the missing details about that fateful night at the railroad station.

She had been waiting with Luke on the platform. They watched train after train, loaded with workers, hired to clear the rubble of the umpteenth bombardment, zoom by. Some trains stopped for just a minute, letting passengers off. Each time a few lucky ones got on. Loek, anxious to get home, told her, "I have so much studying left to do for my accountant's exam in a few days, I absolutely *have* to get on the next train. When the next train rolled in he tried to jump on and missed, falling to his death between the platform and the wheels of the train.

Though devastating, at least we knew the truth. We went through the next few months in a daze. Our original misgivings for having to move to Rotterdam turned into a strong dislike. The only good moments came when we heard the news, caught on a broadcast from London, about allied successes against the Germans. We hoped and prayed for a swift end to all this misery.

My parents, feeling the need for support in their grief, started to go to church. They poured out their hearts to a very compassionate minister. "We want to know if our son is in heaven, we want a sign," they told him. That's when the minister suggested they get in contact with one of his good friends, an elderly lady who held "séances."

My mother had heard that a lot of so-called messages from beyond are in essence facts that the "medium" is familiar with. So during the first session, still very skeptical about the whole affair, she asked for a message from Loek that the medium couldn't have known. After a few moments the following words were spelled out: "People thought you were my older sister." My mother was reassured. That was indeed a compliment strangers had often given her.

As I know many people think séances are a lot of bunk, I want to tell about my own experience the one time I was allowed to "sit in." I was eighteen.

Together with my parents I was led into a semi-dark room. I was a little apprehensive, not knowing what to expect. Besides my family there were a few others present. We were assembled around a heavy oak dining room table. "Put your hands flat on the table top," we were told

For the uninitiated, a spirit from "beyond" makes his or her presence known through the psychic powers of the medium. She goes into a "trance" and tells whose spirit is there to communicate with us. The departed then starts to spell out words, letter by letter, by moving the table up and down. One tap is an A, two taps equals a B etc. It was a long tedious procedure.

As soon as the séance I attended started, the entire table moved towards *me* and started to bang out the words: "You should not do that anymore." I was baffled. My mom, of course, was even more intrigued and yes, worried. "What shouldn't she do anymore?" she wanted to know. Nothing happened for several minutes while I was frantically thinking about what was meant by that admonition. I thought of my playing hookie occasionally, but even Loek had at times written excuses for me. There was total silence. All of a sudden I remembered my secret shopping spree, *going to The Hague* during school hours. The moment that thought went through my mind the table started to go wildly up and down. In other words, yes, that's what was meant.

I cringed. What was going to happen to me now that the spiritual world knew about my misdeeds? Was I going to be doomed to hell? To my intense relief the session continued. I'll never forget that evening. And of course, I had to confess to my parents what I had done.

After a few months of attending these séances my parents quit. Some of the later messages coming through had spelling mistakes in them, very much unlike Loek. It became obvious the medium was influencing the outcome. My mother in the meantime had done some research on spiritualism and decided it was better to leave Loek's soul alone.

Loek van Dalsum
May 9, 1921 - January 14, 1943

CHAPTER 13

Is Liberation Near?

During the summer of 1943, to get away from all the sadness of that year, we spent a few weeks in a small hotel in a pretty village in central Holland. Under the Nazi regime you couldn't just travel as you pleased; for any trip outside a certain distance from your hometown a *permit* was needed.

We were enjoying our vacation when suddenly twelve-year old Toto became deathly ill. She was rushed to the hospital in a nearby city, where the doctors at first diagnosed her with spinal meningitis. My parents heard the dreadful words: "She probably won't last through the night." I can only guess at my parents' reaction to that devastating diagnosis. Just seven months after the death of their oldest, were they now going to lose their youngest child as well?

Toto held on though, proving the doctors wrong. She did have a very serious infection and spent weeks in the hospital. Except for my mother, who stayed close to the hospital, we all went home.

During that time my father wrote her several letters. Among the cache of letters I found almost a life-time later, which I wrote about in a previous chapter, there was one dated September 6, 1943. Besides my dad's concern about Toto's health it contained some interesting tidbits about rationing during that period:

And now a few words about our ration cards. We received a rare candy coupon, which I was able to trade in for chocolates! The occasional coupons for butter are now only for people under 21. I can't find any textile coupons on my card. Please take a look at your card and if there's one for textile buy me some socks at once, as I'm on my last pair. I don't have a coupon for soap either. That one will expire soon, so if you have one, buy the soap there. To my delight we did get a coupon for shaving cream recently. As for meat, even with my meat coupon there was none available anywhere. All I could get was a small piece of liverwurst. I should also tell you that the lining in Hans' winter coat was so torn that it couldn't be repaired. A new lining requires two textile coupons. Any idea how we can manage to get some more of those?

Exactly nine months later, on June 6, 1944, the news we had long been waiting to hear was literally shouted from the rooftops: ALLIED FORCES INVADE NORMANDY! Everybody was jubilant, expecting the war to be over soon. On a broadcast from the BBC we heard how American troops had marched into Paris. The Allies were getting closer and closer. In our minds we already saw the hated Nazis retreating. Just a few more weeks and Holland will be liberated, most Dutchmen thought.

My cautious father had his doubts. He reasoned that the Germans would not be kicked out that easily and that the coming winter might well be very difficult with little food and coal. "I think we should move away from the city as soon as possible. We can move back immediately after the war is over."

Through friends he was able to rent a few inexpensive rooms in a farmhouse in *Putten,* a small rural village about seventy miles north-east of Rotterdam. We had no trouble subletting our apartment, which was a boon to our financial predicament; as it was furnished we received more rent than we paid each month.

We packed what we felt we needed most: clothes of course, but also some luxury items, like my mother's jewelry and well-cared for leather bags, sterling silver objects, sheets, and other hard-to-get household items, all for bartering if the need arose. Last but not least, we took a hockey stick for me, several tennis racquets, and one bicycle. Tires with inner tubes had been unavailable for years, so Pop had outfitted its wheels with thick, hard rubber strips. We were lucky some trains were still running for the general public; a few months later the Germans started to monopolize them for transporting troops and weapons.

After our arrival in Putten in mid July we settled into a new routine. It was still summer vacation and we children actually enjoyed ourselves. Fourteen-year old Hans played soccer with the local kids, while I played hockey and tennis.

While playing hockey I met several other young people I started to hang out with. One guy, Luther Kortlang, became my boyfriend—a summer romance! Frankly it was more serious from his side than mine but we had good times with the whole group.

While visiting at our house, Luther often talked about the future. He mentioned he had recently graduated from college with a degree in Colonial Agriculture and wanted to start his own plantation on the island of Java in the Dutch East Indies after the war.

My father immediately became alarmed upon hearing this. Fearing I might marry Luther and move to the other end of the globe, he started to tell me horror stories about living in the Indies. "You will have cockroaches sitting on the rim of your tea cup," was one of his favorite topics. I had no idea where he got that information but, being pretty sure I wasn't going anywhere soon, didn't want to argue with him.

During one of our get-togethers with the hockey players one of the girls brought an *ouija board* with her. Just for fun we started to ask the kind of questions, which could only have a *Yes* or *No* answer. As a response to, "Will I live a long life" we all got a *Yes* answer except for Luther. He tried again and it came up *No* a second time. "Oh well," we said to make him feel better, "it's just a game." We never tried it again.

It slowly began to dawn on me, listening to my friends' conversations, that all of them were heavily involved in the Dutch *underground* movement. Not long after, Luther took me to the hiding place, somewhere deep in the forest, of other resistance fighters who could no longer live out in the open as they were wanted by the Germans. One of their tasks was to sabotage German troop transportation, like blowing up bridges and railroads. They also provided vital intelligence regarding German strength of forces to the Allies as they came nearer. Luther, as it became obvious, was part of the liaison between them and the outside world. One month later when it became too dangerous for the fighters to be seen around town, Luther had to go in hiding as well.

Our new "home" consisted of a very small, cramped living room. There was a WC (a tiny room with a toilet), two bedrooms, and a kitchen. No tub or showers. We learned how to take "sailors' baths."

We didn't really mind this primitive living, as we felt it was just for a short time. The war was going to be over soon! We excitedly followed the advances of the allied troops, aired in great detail by the BBC. We often went to a neighbor's house to hear the latest news, always careful no German soldiers found out about the clandestine radio.

Early in September I went to yet another high school, five miles away. When luck was with me I hitched a ride on a horse-drawn buggy or on the back of someone's bicycle, but I often had to walk. After winter weather arrived a few months later, that trip proved to be impossible for teachers and students alike. I received homework assignments for one month at a time in each subject. When finished it was up to me to track down each teacher, discuss the work and get a new assignment.

In the meantime, good news about the war continued. Antwerp and Brussels in Belgium were free! Beginning on September 17 the southern part of Holland, town by town, was liberated. The Allies were getting so close...we could almost *taste* freedom. People started to prepare for liberation parties; red, white and blue paraphernalia was taken out of the closets. Our liberators were only forty miles away...thirty-five... thirty—the excitement became palpable. Then suddenly— DISASTER!

Because of a military blunder the allied forces were stopped at Arnhem, a mere *twenty-three miles* from Putten. The book, later made into a movie: "A Bridge Too Far," tells about that period in history in great detail.

We were devastated. No celebrations, no end to this miserable war. Our situation soon got worse, much worse. At the end of September 1944, the Dutch underground attacked a car filled with (what they were told) top-ranking Nazi officials. One was killed and several were wounded. After that event life in Putten would never be the same.

The "Moffen," as the Dutch called the Nazis, couldn't leave this murder unpunished. They ordered everyone living in the village—men, women and children—to come to the marketplace to get what they called a *lecture.*

It so happened, that a friend of my father's had just arrived from Rotterdam on his bike, in search of food to take home. "Let's go over and see what they have to say," he suggested. "No way," my father answered, ever suspicious of what the Germans might do to men of any age during mass assemblies. He decided to hide in a dry creek bed. The friend, curious to see what it was all about, accompanied my mom, Hans, and me. As Toto was sick, my mother got permission for her to stay home.

As soon as we reached the marketplace women and children were herded into a church while the men, five hundred in all, stayed outside. We sat there for almost four hours, fearful about what might happen. I was scared to death as I remembered a story from the year before about a church in

Poland, filled with women and children that the Germans had blown to pieces. Were we all going to die? My mother was having the same thoughts and, trying to save at least one more of her children, asked a guard (she spoke excellent German) if Hans could go home to take care of his sick sister. The guard let Hans go but not without a warning to be very careful outside.

It soon became obvious this had not been one of my mother's brighter ideas. The roads were deserted. When a couple of soldiers saw Hans walking by himself they started shooting at him. He quickly dove into some bushes and managed to get home taking a detour through the forest.

At long last, to our great relief, orders were shouted out to let us all go. Outside we found an empty square. Where were the men? Soon we discovered the devastating news that all five hundred, regardless of age, had been loaded into railroad cars and transported to work camps in Germany. A few men had been able to jump off the train while still in Holland but of the rest *only three came back alive* after the war was over. It was one of the worst disasters in Holland during German occupation. We speculated that my father's friend never got a chance to explain that he didn't even live in Putten.

The villagers' punishment didn't stop there. Next, the entire population was ordered to leave town, as the Germans were planning to burn two hundred houses at random during the night. All of us, my father included, quickly gathered a few clothes and set out for the other side of the town limit. Was it safe for my father to be seen outside now? Yes, relatively so. At age 56 he was considered too old to work in German factories.

The local farmers outside of Putten were very cooperative; they opened up their haylofts for everyone, and cooked big pots of oatmeal. We settled in as best we could but sleep was impossible. Allied planes flew over all night long, most likely wondering about the many burning buildings. At one point we heard shooting. That's when my mother became hysterical. Feeling it was getting too dangerous upstairs, she ordered us all to the first floor. Everyone climbed down except my father. After five minutes of waiting my mother shouted,

"Pop, come down, right now!" My father replied, "Don't get excited, I'll come as soon as I find my *slippers.*" Mom now started to scream, "Listen to that man, we may all get killed but he's looking for his slippers." At that point the rest of us burst out laughing; the situation was just too crazy. And why he had even bothered to bring slippers defied all logic.

The next morning we returned home. To our relief we found our farmhouse unharmed. What the Germans had burned down were about one hundred beautiful mansions and an equal number of small laborers' houses, belonging to poor people with little or no fire insurance.

Many years after the war it came to light what had happened before the Nazis decided to send the five hundred men away: The Mayor of Putten had been ordered by the High German Command to select ten hostages from among the villagers to be executed for the deadly act of the resistance. Though the Mayor was pro-German he also had many friends among the people in Putten. He told the Germans he couldn't arbitrarily pick ten of his friends to be put to death. That's when the Germans switched to alternative punishment, resulting in the death of five hundred.

After this horrible incident, life in general became much more difficult. Soon electricity was cut off and food rations cut down to almost nothing. We did have gas but only from 5 to 7 in the afternoon. Our money situation was equally bad. The proceeds from our house in Scheveningen, together with my father's cashed-in life insurance policy, were practically all gone. We kept a jar with a few guilders in case of an emergency and for those (rare) times food became available on our ration cards.

We didn't skip *Sinterklaas*, though. All the presents we gave each other were hand-made from materials we found or got from friends. The daughter of a wealthy family nearby gave me a ball of paper twine she found in her attic. I hand-wove (like macramé) a shopping bag for my mother from that material. As lipstick was impossible to get anymore, Hans, as a gag gift, made me a giant lipstick from old newspapers, painted red. And like any good Sinterklaas present, each and every one was accompanied by a funny poem. The evening was a huge success and brought some much-needed entertainment for our family. My mother added to the excitement by baking syrup cookies.

Christmas went by in a blur. We didn't even bother with a tree. The New Year, 1945, was rung in with very little fanfare. Our only thought was: would this year bring the end to the war?

CHAPTER 14

The Hunger Winter

One of the gifts I received for my twentieth birthday, January 2, 1945, was a soft-cover notebook with what we called "war paper": thin, unbleached scratch paper. It was a rare find as most stores had closed their doors due to the fact there was nothing to sell.

I decided to make the notebook into a *diary,* writing down interesting tidbits and events that took place during that most unusual winter.

Our days were primarily filled with finding food and fuel. Except for Toto, who was too young to venture out on her own, we each set out daily in different directions to finagle food from neighboring farmers. Hans found a small farm run by two elderly sisters. He called them "ouwe wijfjes," literally translated, *little old women.* Hans was a cute boy, a real charmer. The sisters got a kick out of him and promised him a pound of butter, which they churned in their kitchen, and a liter of milk once a week, in return for some wood chopping. Their operation was not the cleanest in the world and we soon discovered the butter contained some tiny black strips. On closer examination we realized they were insect legs—fly legs most likely. Of course that didn't deter us from using it. We simply called it our "poten boter," Dutch for *leg butter.*

My mom was the "peddler." When getting to a farmhouse she gave her spiel: "Do you have some food to trade?

I have ersatz (imitation) coffee, salt, children's boots and kitchen towels." She was usually very successful. For a brand-new chamois cloth she got twenty pounds of rye flour. For a skirt I had worn for three years and Toto for two she was given butter and eggs. Two pairs of inexpensive earrings were traded for four pounds of oatmeal and two pounds of syrup. That syrup was a real bonus, as sugar was impossible to get.

I tried my best trading a few items from my meager belongings. For a brooch I once bought on sale for twenty-five cents, I got a pound of butter. My expertise however, was in checking the movements of harvesting machines. Most farmers didn't have the means to buy their own machinery. Instead, they contracted with outsiders to do the work for them. On those occasions the farmers became quite generous: the first fifty visitors got a bag full of wheat or rye (or whatever they were harvesting) at ten cents a pound. (On the black market that would have cost at least ten guilders, approximately $3.) It used to be the poor people who followed the machines, but during the *hunger winter* even the wealthy tried to get some of this grain.

To do his share of gathering food, my father would ride his bike (with the hard-rubber tires) for days, trying to locate his old customers, butcher shop owners in particular. He would put an old suitcase on his bike and come back with meat and flour that he had traded for a leather handbag or a piece of sterling. To preserve the meat our landlord smoked it for us, ensuring we could use it for many weeks to come. Next we put the flour in what we considered a safe place. Unfortunately the *mice* were hungry as well. One day while removing some of the flour to make bread we found half a dozen baby mice that had suffocated in the middle of the sack. We changed its name to "muizen tarwe," *mice wheat*. Though not exactly very appetizing we couldn't afford to throw all of it out. We tossed the mice and kept the wheat.

At the end of each week the person who had brought in the most food got a special treat. We called it the "Nobel sandwich." It consisted of a slice of real bread with thick butter and a fried egg. A baker in town made the bread. As compensation for his baking we had to hand in double the ingredients. The bread we normally ate was a concoction my father had figured out by trial and error: stovetop boiled bread. Not great but definitely filling. Once two "trekkers," rang our doorbell asking if they could spend the night at our house. (The word *trekkers* described hungry people from the cities who walked or rode their bikes for days, trying to find food.) As we had barely enough room for our own family we told them where they might be able to find a place. Before they left, my father gave them a loaf of his boiled bread. They thanked us profusely and said excitedly, "That will be our food for an entire week!"

Our farmer landlord occasionally slaughtered a pig to provide meat for his family. On such occasions he gave us some *blood sausage*, which consisted of pure blood with a thickening ingredient. I know it sounds awful but tasted pretty good when fried.

Once in a while our city fathers provided free meat. This was a most peculiar operation. Every family in the village was issued a number. Hitler's big shiny tanks and trucks were a thing of the past. Close to defeat, the army now had to use old horses for transportation. When allied planes spotted those strange troop movements, they often started to shoot. Whenever they killed a horse, its carcass was brought to city hall and cut into pieces. Next, the *town crier* made his rounds, ringing a bell and yelling out loud which numbers were to receive a portion of the horse. Arriving at the town square you couldn't help but see a big garbage can with the horse's head sticking out. Not too appealing but who cared? It was *meat*. Coming from an old horse it was terribly tough and had to be cooked for days to become edible.

Early in February Hans brought home a... *pig*, which he "found" near a German compound. It was so little and emaciated he could easily hide it under his coat. To be of any use to us we had to fatten it up but that left a big dilemma: "With what?" We fed it some potato peels and a few other things unfit for human consumption. After a month we realized the futility of our efforts and had our landlord slaughter it. Lots of *baby-back ribs*, but hardly any meat.

One of our neighbors was a rich French woman, who somehow had gotten stuck in Putten during that winter. We called her *Madame*. She often gave us ersatz "tea," either a powder or tablet made from berries, leaves and even potatoes. On her request, whenever we had more eggs than we could eat, we sold them to her—at an inflated price— for some much needed cash.

The winter of 1945 was unusually cold. Though our tiny living room came supplied with a potbelly stove we had to provide our own wood. Hans and I became the wood cutters. Twice a week we took a cart Pop had made and went out into the state-owned forests to cut trees with a hand saw. It was, of course, illegal, so my mom came along as *lookout*. We tried to do all our cutting during the forest rangers' dinnertime.

As we were inexperienced—and a little scared—we cut just thin little trees at first. Even felling those made an enormous racket. Next we had to cut them into pieces to make them fit on our cart. Freshly cut, it was "green" (wet) wood and hard to light. Newspapers were a thing of the past. Even with the dry kindling we gathered it often took close to an hour to get a decent fire going. The thin trees soon proved to burn too fast, so we got bolder and cut thicker ones. Hans became so good at sawing trees that he often helped neighbors with that task, in exchange for food or salt.

Postal delivery was hit and miss. Occasionally we would receive a letter or postcard from the cities. Most letters were hand-carried by friends from The Hague, who actually *walked* or rode their bikes for days in search of food. In comparison to what they were experiencing, we were not that bad off. What follows are some excerpts from those letters. One was from a friend of my mother's who had grown up in luxury:

There's no more gas or electricity and we simply can't buy anything anymore, even on the black market. Millions are starving and thousands of babies are dying from a shortage of baby food. New mothers can get a ration of one pail of hot water twice a week to wash their babies.

Can you imagine that I, a woman who always ate the finest food, now stand in line for hours to get a bowl of watery soup? Next to me stood the wife of a doctor. We're all in the same boat.

My father's bookkeeper wrote at the end of January:

Not only do we have practically no food but we ran out of coal as well. We have actually started to burn our furniture to stay warm. First came our bookcase, next an armoire and soon we'll be burning tables and chairs. Some of our friends have cut the balconies off their houses for firewood.

A new ordinance just came out that anyone trying to cut down trees or benches from the parks and forests or remove railroad ties, will be shot on the spot.

From one of my school friends: *An aborted V-2 missile fell close to our home. The house is near collapse, without a roof, windows, or doors. It's a miracle all of us survived with only a few cuts and bruises. As for food, we've been eating tulip bulbs instead of potatoes.*

I should mention here that the Dutch have always been big potato eaters. When I was growing up my mother would occasionally make a rice or macaroni casserole dish for dinner but the *standard* meal consisted of meat or chicken, potatoes with gravy, and vegetables. Being forced to forego potatoes was a real disaster for many. Trying to get some kind of substitute during the winter of '45 many people descended on the huge tulip fields located north of The Hague, yanked the bulbs from the grounds, and took them home to eat.

When we heard about those hardships in the cities, we were even more grateful my father had had the foresight to move to the countryside. At the same time we envied the Dutch in the southern part of Holland who had been liberated over six months ago.

Grocery stores in town opened their doors whenever new ration cards were issued. This didn't amount to much; we were lucky to get some potatoes, beans, matches, a liter of milk, a small piece of cheese, and a loaf of bread once in a while. As I mentioned earlier, imported items became unavailable shortly after the beginning of the war unless you were willing and able to pay scandalously high prices on the black market. But by 1945, even daily necessities like soap, shampoo, toothpaste, toilet paper and the like, were non-existent. As for women's special needs: sanitary napkins were simply not available. We just bunched some rags together, which we washed in cold water and re-used.

The few stores that remained open became trading centers. Their display windows announced items being offered for bartering: two bed sheets for ten kilos of potatoes, three yards of dress material for twenty pounds of rye or wheat, a pair of size 9 leather men's shoes for five pounds of sugar, and many more such offerings.

Ingenious Hans had another brilliant idea. Several people had started to grow their own tobacco. After harvesting and cutting it they needed a special type of paper to roll cigarettes. Hans heard through the grapevine that a former office supply store owner still had stacks of "onion skin" paper for sale (used in the olden days together with carbon paper to make copies when typing a letter). He bought an entire ream for one guilder and proceeded to cut each sheet neatly into twenty "cigarette papers." He sold each package of twenty for one guilder to the tobacco growers—a huge profit! One week he sold *sixty* packages.

By the end of February our food supplies had dwindled precariously. We had nothing more to trade and the farmers practically closed their doors because of the thousands of trekkers from the cities who came begging. Many starving people stole food right from the fields. Some city folks walked for days, pushing hand carts on wooden wheels, hoping to get them filled with something edible and durable. The lucky ones who managed to get a cart-full of potatoes had a new problem: the load was often so heavy that the cart collapsed before they returned home. Fortunately there always seemed to be a Good Samaritan to help with repairs. As for us, we only had a few regular places left (like the old sisters) where we were promised some milk, butter and eggs once a week.

According to a story making the rounds in Putten there was an elderly woman who had nothing left to trade. She looked around her house, searching for anything of value to the farmers. Suddenly her eye caught her white, crocheted bedspread. Hmm, she thought, I could unravel that spread and knit children's socks. She proceeded to do just that. After a few days of constant knitting she ended up with five pair plus one single sock. Off she went to the nearest farmhouse. The farmer's wife loved the five pairs of socks and gave the woman quite a bit of food in trade. Then she asked, "You don't, by chance, have any more yarn?" Yes, there was the additional, lone sock. "I'll trade you that too," came the wife's enthusiastic reply. "You see, I'm going to unravel the socks and crochet myself a bedspread."

When the snow melted in early March our situation brightened. We could now go into the woods to pick blueberries and chanterelles, easy recognizable and edible mushrooms. They tasted good fried, even better with scrambled eggs. Another advantage of the warmer weather: we could finally burn our very dirty, worn-out winter clothes.

Although the war was winding down, bad news kept coming. First we heard that my grandmother's home in The Hague was destroyed during a British bombardment. She had just left for a walk when bombs, meant for German targets, were dropped. Though it was a miracle she survived, at the age of sixty-five she suddenly found herself with nothing left but the clothes on her back.

Another piece of news was much worse: Luther, my last-summer boyfriend, was executed by the Germans. Shortly after the war I heard the sad details from his sister Annie:

> *Luther, considered an important member of the Dutch underground, was sought by the Germans. When they were unable to find him they went to his parents' house late in January and arrested his (non-involved) father and brother. They left a message with his mother stating, that as soon as Luther turned himself in, his father and brother would be set free. Though obviously a trap, Luther did turn himself in and was imprisoned. After many interrogations about the Dutch underground he was executed. His father and brother, in a different prison, were shot to death not long after. Annie was summoned to the various prisons to identify the bodies of her three family members.*
>
> *It also became known that Luther had a chance to escape with several other prisoners. Luther, fearing for the life of his father and brother if he did so, refused to go along. The two escaped prisoners made it to safety.*

Friends listening to BBC broadcasts brought us good news at last: "The Germans can't last another two months. The Allies will be meeting the Russians in two days!" Daily we saw hundreds of British bombers fly over, heading for Germany. Other Allied planes tossed out flyers for the German soldiers to read: how to capitulate, treatment of POWs, etc.

Victory and liberation were near. We could hardly wait for our dreams of freedom to become reality.

On a hunch, in July of 2007, I "googled" Luther's name and to my astonishment found a long article in Dutch, telling in great detail what exactly had happened to him during the spring of 1945. His execution took place on March 2 and posthumously Luther, his father, and brother were awarded the "Verzetsherdenkingskruis" (Memorial Resistance Cross). A TV broadcast about his life was aired in Holland on May 4, 2007.

CHAPTER 15

Holland Is Free!

It was deadly quiet on the afternoon of April 17, 1945. What was left of the German army in Putten, a disheveled group of old men, sprinkled with a few boys in their early teens, hastily left town that morning. Some fled on foot, some on bicycles without tires, others pushing handcarts with broken wheels—the last traces of the once mighty *Deutsche Wehrmacht.* A few of the soldiers carried signs: "We rather die than become slaves."

Shortly after midnight we heard a tremendous explosion. We all raced to the fall-out shelter our landlord had built a few years earlier. Just before we closed its door a very young boy in Nazi uniform appeared from the surrounding bushes. "Please can I stay with you?" he begged, "I'm just a kid, I never wanted to fight." He showed us the pamphlet he had found on how to surrender and explained that as soon as the Allies arrived he would turn himself in. Once inside the shelter the boy told us he was only fifteen. With the Germans fighting on two fronts, boys as young as fourteen had been ordered to serve. We told the boy not to fear being taken prisoner and taught him how to say: "I surrender."

All night long we heard grenades zooming over, whistling through the air. Nobody slept. Suddenly, at dawn: an eerie silence. It was deadly quiet. Hans and Pop cautiously went exploring. They soon reported back: Lots of caved-in houses, dead Germans, guns and ammunition strewn around. The rest of us wanted to take a look but loudspeakers ordered everyone to clear the streets. *"The Canadians are coming!"* blared through the town.

We waited in great anticipation for what was to come. Suddenly, a shout, "There they are!" In the distance we saw row upon row of the most modern gleaming tanks. In contrast to the sight of pathetic looking German soldiers only a few days ago, we glanced in awe at the Canadian troops, young and gorgeous creatures, tall and suntanned. Though some tanks crisscrossed the outlying fields in search of fleeing soldiers, the majority headed straight for town. My father hurried back to the shelter, took the German boy by the arm and said, "Quick, put your hands up and turn yourself in." The kid was scared to death but did as he was told.

Downtown it felt like a parade; everyone was waving and cheering. A tall, white-gloved MP was directing traffic while tank crews threw chocolate bars and gum to the people lining the streets; it truly was a sight to behold. We were all wearing red white and blue. Every so often we pinched each other; was this really happening or was it just a dream?

Amidst all this jubilation, collaborators, Dutch people who had befriended the Germans, were picked up and put on display for all to see. Dutch girls who had dated German soldiers were yanked from their homes and brought to the town center to have their hair shaved off. Everyone cheered the barbers on.

We just could not get enough of the scene; nobody felt like going home. Just listening to English spoken all around us was thrilling. We slept wonderfully well that night, knowing that our five-year ordeal was over.

Most of the Canadian army went on to liberate subsequent towns. A few sections, however, set up camp not far from our house. While walking by one of the camps two soldiers called us over. "You want some fresh bread?" they asked. Then they proceeded to give us corned beef, tea, and sugar! Wanting to continue speaking English I asked, "Do you want to meet a Dutch family?" That's exactly what these soldiers, after many months of fighting, needed. They gladly accepted. One young soldier in particular, *Eddie*, became a regular visitor. Each time before he left he would ask, "Is there anything you would like me to bring tomorrow?" We all shouted at once, "Soap, chocolate, peanut butter." My parents added to the list: "Coffee, shaving cream."

A few days before my father's 57th birthday, May 2, we asked Eddie if he could bring a pack of cigarettes as a surprise gift. He brought a box containing five hundred! My father couldn't believe his good fortune.

Dances were organized in the school gym. It was heaven to listen to American music again. We quickly learned not only many of the new popular songs but also how to *jitterbug*.

Amidst all this happiness we sympathized with our friends and relatives back home, in the western part of Holland, who weren't yet liberated. We were thrilled to hear that the Germans allowed British planes to drop steel drums with food on the big cities for the starving population. British pilots literally fought for the honor of being part of this food drop.

On April 30 Hitler committed suicide. A few days later Germany surrendered. For Holland the war ended on May 5, 1945.

New festivities followed this long awaited news. We all went downtown, kissing friends and strangers alike. Arm in arm we danced through the streets, singing patriotic songs and shouting, "Long live the queen." Resistance fighters we hadn't seen in a long time reappeared and joined the party.

That same day, over 5200 miles away, the man who was to become my life's partner, turned 25. There was no celebration for him; he had to endure another four months under dismal circumstances, before liberation became a reality for him as well. Our first meeting wouldn't take place until five years later.

After the initial excitement was over, we started to think about going back to Scheveningen or The Hague. In order to find a place to live we *had* to be right there. My parents' friends and neighbors from the Zeeweg, who had moved to The Hague, invited us to come and stay with them until we found a house. This left just one problem: How would we get there?

At an officers' dance shortly after liberation I had met a very nice Canadian captain, Paul, who was in charge of a motor pool. Unlike some of the over-sexed soldiers, Paul was a very sweet guy with a wife back home he often talked about. He had mentioned to me, if we ever needed transportation, to let him know. When he left Putten, he told me where they were going to be for the next two or three weeks: *Zwolle,* a city about thirty miles from Putten. As there was no other way to get home soon, it was decided I would try to find Paul.

Getting to Zwolle was one thing, but once I arrived there I had to find out where, in a city of several hundred thousand people, his particular section was stationed. After a lot of searching and a bit of luck I located him and told him what we needed. Paul promised to be at our home in Putten two days later and to my intense relief offered to have one of his men give me a ride back in a jeep.

We packed our belongings—which didn't amount to much—and waited. At the appointed time a huge van drove up. We laughed; it was big enough to move fifty households. The driver helped us load our stuff and we all climbed in, anxious to leave Putten, with so many bad memories, behind. We were finally going back to a normal life, back to civilization!

CHAPTER 16

Hitchhiking

It took a while after the end of the war before trains started running regular schedules again. Literally everyone, young and old, rode a bike in Holland. If it was raining you just put on a poncho. It was a way of life. I went everywhere pedaling my bike, including going to work. Yes, *work!* In August of 1945 I had gotten a job at the ANWB, the Dutch equivalent of the AAA. Though the pay was low at first I was promised quick raises if they liked my work.

To me it was a dream job. I worked with just one woman, an older, native French speaker. As traffic regulations, border requirements, and a host of other legalities had changed over the five war years, we had to put together a booklet for motorists driving to other countries in Europe.

We corresponded with all countries open to car traffic, sending a long list of questions and asking for their input. The letters were in French, it being the most universal, diplomatic language at that time. The two of us had a great time doing this work. We were thrilled when our final masterpiece was printed. My salary by that time had doubled.

The above, however, is not the main reason for including this story. There was a special incentive attached to working for the ANWB. As membership had gone down to almost zero during the war, they offered its employees one whole extra day off with pay for every new member they signed up. No insignificant perk!!

To go anywhere outside the city, the only mode of transportation was by hitchhiking. Everybody hitchhiked; there was absolutely no danger attached. The lucky people who could afford to drive a car were mostly doctors, businessmen, and truck drivers.

I don't quite remember where I went on weekends but my friends and I, after so much confinement during the war, went all over the place. We stood by the side of the road, sticking out our thumb. It never took long to get a ride—drivers were happy to pick us up.

An ingenious scheme started to form in my mind: *these drivers could benefit from membership in the ANWB!* So I told them where I worked and related what they were missing if they weren't a member yet. I always took application forms with me and often, by the time they dropped me off, I had made a new member. Within six months I had earned an entire extra month of paid vacation.

One driver got back at me, though. He was a big shot with the Red Cross. After signing up he said, "Okay, now it's *my* turn. How about a donation to the Red Cross?" What could I do? Reluctantly, I handed him a five-guilder bill, roughly half a day's pay.

Even when trains went back to normal, we kept thumbing rides for many years; it was fun, cheap, and totally safe.

CHAPTER 17

Nylon Stockings

Slowly, life started to get back to normal. My father found a job and through my mother's perseverance, we managed to find a three-story house for rent in a nice neighborhood. Food, clothes, and gasoline, though still rationed, became more plentiful. Post-war trade relations with the States, however, were still in its infancy.

Suddenly we heard about this new American invention, a godsend for women: *nylon stockings*. It was on every woman's lips—they were supposed to be comfortable, beautiful and almost indestructible. However, the crucial adjective describing this miracle was: *unavailable*. Sad as it was, you simply couldn't get them unless you had some *connections*. Yes, they were available on the *black market,* at a price. They were smuggled in I suppose.

Every woman craved to own a pair, including *me.* Through the grapevine we heard about "addresses," where you could make an appointment to come and buy a pair, all very hush-hush. At long last, I found such a treasured place. At the appointed time I went to the back door of an old house in a pretty shabby neighborhood. (These illegal operations never seemed to be in nice areas.) After stating my size (this was long before one-size-fits-all stretch nylons) a box was brought out; two colors to choose from. I finally became the proud owner of a pair of nylon stockings. It cost me an entire week's salary.

These early nylons were indeed very strong. Though gorgeous to the women who had never seen anything like it, they were of a much thicker gauge than later ones. But accidents did happen, runs did appear in them. A whole new cottage industry arose: repairing runs in nylons, restoring them to look like new. Even when nylons in Holland became available and cheaper, the frugal Dutch had their nylons repaired until well into the 1950s.

I remember an incident seven years later, while living in California. I had just snagged one of my new stockings and asked a friend where I could find a repair shop. She looked at me as if I had come from Mars. "You want your nylons *repaired*? You can't be serious! Just toss them and buy a new pair," she advised. That was not the way I was brought up. I put the hose in an envelope and sent them to Holland for repair.

CHAPTER 18

A Failed Romance and It's Aftermath

During the last year of the war there had been a severe scarcity of young men. Now at long last, my social life started to pick up. I joined a new tennis and hockey club. I loved playing hockey, running around on the grass, and then afterwards meeting with friends in the clubhouse.

I went out on dates, going to dances and movies or, in the winter, went ice-skating on the Dutch canals and lakes. As with many girls my age, we were all waiting for that "tall, dark, and handsome" guy.

At one of our evening get-togethers with my hockey club in the winter of 1947, I noticed a dashing man I had never seen before. He was tall, good-looking, with dark-brown eyes. A friend told me he was an old member of our club, who, as captain in the Dutch army was stationed in the Dutch East Indies (which later became Indonesia). I'll refer to him as PQ.

It didn't take long before he struck up a conversation with me. To my disappointment I heard he had only three weeks leave left in Holland. We talked for hours. At the end of the evening he asked if he could walk me home.

It was love at first sight; I fell madly in love with him and he with me. I had never been head over heels in love before. We went out almost every evening, usually to a quiet place where we could talk. Clothes became a problem—I had so little to wear. As luck would have it, a package arrived from an uncle in California with two dresses my size. PQ was always in uniform.

Too soon his leave came to an end. Since he assured me he'd come back to Holland in three months, our separation didn't seem so bad. Though we hadn't gone beyond kissing we talked about a future together. Looking back, I realize I really knew very little about him and had rarely seen him interact with friends or his family.

We exchanged long letters. After three months he wrote me that leave would be impossible to get for at least a year. One year turned to two. That's when his letters started to get strange. He had been transferred to Saigon in French Indo-China (now Vietnam). Sometimes I had the feeling he was drunk when he wrote, but hey, I was in love, wasn't I? In retrospect I think I was *in love with being in love*. He did ask me to go see his parents, a very friendly old couple. I immediately found out PQ had lied about his age. Instead of a five-year difference I was told he was eight years older than me. This made me wonder....

When PQ finally returned to Holland he had been away for twenty-seven months. And...while stationed in Saigon *he had met a French woman*. Our reunion was a bitter disappointment for me. After a month he went back to Saigon.

I felt broken-hearted at first. Then something happened that made me a believer in destiny. If I had never met PQ, I would probably have gotten married to some other Dutchman. And of course, I would never have met PQ's mother. *She* was the one who told me about the fantastic secretarial jobs at Dutch embassies and legations in foreign countries. Unfamiliar with those opportunities—they sounded almost too good to be true—I made some inquiries. In September of 1949 I sent a job application to the Dutch State Department.

Within two weeks I got an interview: "We have an opening for a secretary starting mid December in *Lisbon, Portugal* you would be suited for. However, there's one requirement you don't have: stenography. Do you think you could learn shorthand in Dutch, French, and English in the next ten weeks?" "Of course," I stammered, almost too excited to talk. I got the job on that condition. They didn't test me on any other skills. The fact that I typed with only four fingers (hunt-and-peck) didn't seem to matter. I later heard why they had been so anxious to hire me; my predecessor in Lisbon had been a rather old, frumpy woman. Ada, my roommate-to-be, had written the State Department an urgent message: *Please send me somebody young and cheerful this time.*

Now came the challenge—I immediately had to start taking lessons in stenography. As regular classes would be much too slow, I went to a private tutor, three and four times a week. I lived and breathed shorthand, becoming practically obsessed, transcribing in my mind literally everything I read and heard. It took me eight weeks to become an expert. Even before I got my diplomas I received my two-year contract and a plane ticket to Lisbon. *LISBON!* It sounded so exotic, so romantic!

I left on December 11, 1949—my *first flight.* Ada, my soon-to-be good friend, met me at the airport. I stepped off the plane with a hockey stick in one hand and a tennis racquet in the other. An entirely new life started for me.

Ada and I shared an old apartment with a great view on the Tagus River. The only drawback was an army of cockroaches crawling around. Work wasn't hard: from 10 to 1, two hours for lunch (so that the big shots could have their sumptuous lunches) and then again from 3 to 6. Domestic help was very affordable. We had a maid who did all our grocery shopping, cleaning, ironing, and cooking. I had so few suitable clothes that I immediately borrowed against future pay to have new dresses made. It's hard to believe, but there was no ready-to-wear available in Portugal.

I soon started to look for a hockey club. As most Portuguese women were non-athletic, I joined a British club. Though under normal circumstances always polite and somewhat reserved, as soon as these Englishmen stepped on a hockey field they became maniacs. I could not believe what I saw: guys and girls—yes, co-ed hockey—were running around on the field, wildly swinging their sticks, breaking every possible rule. I was just about to quit when one guy stepped in front of me to get the ball and hit me in the forehead with his stick. Blood all over the place. Suddenly the British politeness returned. The game was stopped and all attention was on me. They took me to the hospital for stitches.

No more hockey for me! Ada and I started to concentrate on tennis. I found it funny that people in Portugal thought I was a good player. Back home I had won exactly *one* C tournament, the lowest there was. Hans had won the Dutch National tennis championships four or five times, while Toto was youth champion once. Both Hans and Toto played at Wimbledon. I was considered just a mediocre player at best. In Lisbon, however, I became a sought-after player, which caused great hilarity among my Dutch family.

I had the last laugh. Tennis was the next link in my life's chain. Without tennis I would never have met John.

As for my *failed romance,* had I married PQ, I would have become a widow at a very young age; he died in 1953 during routine surgery.

CHAPTER 19

Love and Marriage

The date was Saturday, May 27, 1950. It was a day I will never forget.

"Paula, I'd like you to meet my good friend, John Boswell." Those words, spoken by South African artist Siegfried Hahn, changed both our lives forever. I was twenty-five and John had just turned thirty.

The meeting took place at the terrace café of the "Estadio Nacional," a tennis stadium in the town of *Cruz Quebrada*, a short train ride from Lisbon. Siegfried had just finished giving John a tennis lesson while I had been playing a few sets with Ada.

I looked up at a tall, broad-shouldered hunk of a man with twinkling blue eyes. We shook hands. Great smile, I thought. My second observation was about his hands and fingers; it struck me how well-groomed they were, with immaculately manicured nails. No *bells and whistles*, but he seemed like a nice guy.

The four of us had a soda and chatted for a while. When we were about ready to leave John asked, "Are you girls coming back next Saturday?" Ada wasn't sure but I told him we probably would.

It didn't take me long to convince Ada to go a week later. On our train ride to the tennis courts I was thinking about the cute American, wondering if I would see him again. On arrival I noticed he was already there, hitting the ball with Siegfried. They waved at us. "See you later at the café," John shouted.

After playing for about an hour we met again for a drink. Ada excitedly talked about her upcoming vacation trip, going to places she'd never seen before. John looked at me and said, "So Paula, you're going to be alone for a while. How about going out to dinner with me one evening?" Not wanting to sound like a pushover I answered, "I'll have to check my schedule. Why don't you give me a call?"

Our first date was on June 9. I hadn't seen much of Lisbon's nightlife yet, but John knew every nook and cranny. "I think you'd like the *Feira Popular*. If you don't we'll go somewhere else," he said. The Feira Popular turned out to be a summer-long amusement park with lots of quaint places to eat, game booths, rides, and best of all, various open-air dance floors.

We had a wonderful time and learned a lot about each other. I soon discovered John had a great sense of humor. Moreover, I felt comfortable being in his company, *I could totally be myself,* different from other dates where I had often felt I was expected to act a certain way.

Later that evening we went dancing. Another surprise: John was an excellent dancer. We slow-danced cheek-to-cheek. John felt like a big teddy bear, with his arms wrapped around me. When he finally took me home I knew this could be the beginning of something special. However, thinking about my failed romance in Holland, which had started out with mutual *love at first sight,* I didn't want to rush into things.

Many more dates followed. Besides being funny and compassionate, John gave me a feeling of self-worth I had never known before. "You have so much on the ball," he once told me. I had no idea what that meant. He used a lot of slang expressions previously unknown to me. "It means you're very smart," he explained. He also thought I was beautiful. At a formal American Embassy ball I wore a new taffeta-and-lace evening dress. "You look *ravishing*," he whispered in my ear. My ego was soaring.

On one of our dates I talked a little about life in Holland under Nazi occupation. Then I casually asked, "Where were *you* during the war?" Startled to see the happy expression on his face of just a few seconds before turn into anger and hurt, I quickly added, "Don't feel you have to tell me if you'd rather not." After a long silence John said in a choked-up voice, "I was a prisoner of war. It's only five years ago and I still find it hard to talk about. Let's change the subject." He took me home early. After kissing me good night he said, "Don't feel bad about asking. I'll tell you more about it another time." How could I not feel bad about it? My heart ached for him, for the obvious pain he was suffering by just the remembrance of those years.

When did I know I was in love with him? I'm not quite sure, but I do remember I felt excited whenever we were together. Each time I discovered new sides of him. I had never known anyone who was so totally unselfish as John, who always thought of *my* pleasure first, wanting *me* to be happy. After several more dates I began to realize that he was the man I had been waiting for all my life. Actually, I was glad it had *not* been love at first sight, for I knew now that I loved him for who he was, and what he stood for—all his good qualities instead of just his looks.

For many months I was waiting to hear him say, "I love you." Through every action he showed me that that was the case. We were considered a couple by our friends, and spent a lot of time together. Yet, those "three little words" were elusive. Was he not completely sure? Was he afraid of commitment? I sometimes wondered, knowing he had had quite a few girlfriends. Through the grapevine I heard he had one or two dates with a Portuguese girl not long before he met me. But I quickly erased those thoughts from my mind—I just had to be patient, give him time.

When I started making plans to visit my family in January of 1951, John told me he had a month vacation coming and would like to come along. I enthusiastically accepted his offer. My mother assured me there was plenty of room for John to stay at our house.

After a one-day stopover in Madrid we flew to Holland, where John was introduced to my family. Except for my dad, who acted somewhat reserved, they all liked him, while John had nothing but praise for the hospitality he was shown.

A few days after our arrival I was sitting in the kitchen, where my mom was cooking dinner. We were talking about John when she suddenly raised the question, "Are the two of you making any plans for the future?" I hesitated. "I don't know, Mom, we haven't really talked about that."

That evening John and I went out for a walk. On our return, just before going back into the house, John asked, "What does your mother think of the two of us?" I told him about our conversation in the kitchen. His immediate reaction was: "Well, didn't you tell her we're going to get married?" I looked at him and shouted, "We are?" to which he replied, "Of course we are, we love each other don't we?" So that was John's marriage proposal, in front of my old house at 45 Van Weede van Dijkveldstraat in The Hague. We went inside and told the family we were *engaged.* After that first declaration he had no trouble telling me over and over how much he loved me.

Shortly after we returned to Lisbon, Ada left for a new assignment in Rio de Janeiro (where she met her future husband, an Englishman). I said goodbye to the old cockroach-riddled apartment and moved to a very small, much more modern and clean place with just enough room for one person.

Soon we began making plans for the future. John, being in charge of the Marine Security Guard, had signed an agreement to remain single while in Portugal. As a matter of fact, only our best friends knew about our future plans. When one of his Marine friends at the Belgium Embassy got serious about a Belgium girl, he was sent back to the U.S. and from there, straight to Korea! We wanted to avoid such a fate at all cost.

John expected to be called back to the States later in the year, about the same time my two-year assignment ended. During 1951 he was promoted to master sergeant.

We both received generous overseas supplements. Knowing that we would earn a lot less in the U.S. we decided to save as much as we could in Portugal. When John asked me if I wanted a diamond ring I told him I would rather save the money to buy necessities for our future home.

John shared a modern apartment with Frank, another Marine. Frank had bought a huge diamond ring for his fiancée. When they got married in the fall of that year they spent every cent they had on their lavish wedding and had to borrow money from John for their honeymoon.

I was more practical, a quality John appreciated in me. "Why spend so much on your wedding?" I told John. "With the money they spent they could have bought a house in the States." John whole-heartedly agreed.

Many years later Siegfried told me about a conversation he had with John before he met me. "Do you think you might like to get married one day?" he had asked, to which John replied, "Yes, but I doubt it will be to an American girl as most of them are just too materialistic."

We saved and saved, becoming downright *frugal*. We did splurge once though, on a sterling tea and coffee service we had seen in one of the little jewelry shops in the *Rua do Ouro* ("Gold Street" in translation). In Portugal at that time you could bargain, even in the most exclusive stores. Each Saturday we went back, trying to get the set for less. After endless weeks, the shop owner relented. Our first important acquisition for our future home! We already started to dream about a home out in the countryside after John retired.

We enjoyed many inexpensive activities during the rest of the year in addition to tennis. When we were lucky enough, someone would give us tickets to the theater. We both loved classical piano concertos, which were performed in a fancy nineteenth century opera house with gilded loges. The dress code was strictly formal; not even a dark suit would do.

Often we would go dancing. Portuguese bands played not just Latin tunes but also the latest pop music from the States, including Doris Day hits, wonderfully romantic songs like *Imagination* and *Bewitched.* Other times we would go to a small, cave-like restaurant famous for the "fado," a lamenting kind of song, typical of Portugal, performed by solemn-looking men or women dressed in black. You could spend an entire evening listening to the songs while sipping cheap—but very good—wine. The Portuguese were so engrossed by the fado singing that they did not tolerate the slightest noise. If you dared even whisper during a performance they would look at you and hiss, "Sssh."

Before I met John, Ada and I had been traipsing all over the hills outside Lisbon. I tried to get John interested in going one Sunday. "No, let's just stay in, I'm tired," was his immediate reply. I kept on pushing and he finally relented, reluctantly. We took a forty-minute train ride to Sintra, the prettiest place I could think of. Soon we were following a trail climbing the hills towards the remains of an old Moorish castle and after that, a centuries-old palace. The farther we got the more enthusiastic John became. "Hey, you didn't tell me it was this beautiful," he kept repeating. "I want to come back and take lots of pictures." No more talk about fatigue—he was feeling great. Many more such trips followed.

On rainy weekends John would organize pictures he had taken and put them in albums, while I knitted argyle socks for him. I had learned that craft from a couple of American girls who were making them for their boyfriends. Made out of nylon yarn they were so strong, John still wore them twenty-five years later.

We also enjoyed the bullfights, which in Portugal are artful, with fantastic ridership, and only a symbolic killing of the bull. They were very different from the often gory spectacle in Spain. Whenever a guest bullfighter from Spain, in the heat of the moment, would mistakenly kill the bull the Portuguese would throw him in jail.

The Marines were not allowed to own a car in Portugal. Occasionally friends from the diplomatic corps, who had access to embassy cars, would invite us for rides outside Lisbon. That's how we came to see many of Portugal's unusual towns and cities. One such town was *Evora*, a walled city dating back to Moorish times, filled with oddities, like a chapel with an entrance sign: "Here lie our bones, waiting for yours." Its entire walls, pillars and ceilings were lined with human bones.

On the evening before his thirty-first birthday, John's friends threw him a big surprise party. The following night, his real birthday, we kept for just the two of us. For that special occasion we went dinner-dancing at a romantic place on the outskirts of Lisbon: the *Alvalade*. Its outside terrace was surrounded by a lovely lake.

It became a memorable, very intimate occasion. We felt closer than ever before. John told me more about himself and opened up about his war experiences. I wrote my mother the following day, *I've never been so happy in all my life.*

A few months before we left Portugal John wanted to have studio portraits taken of me, not only for himself but also to send to his closest relatives. Oh no, that's going to be a disaster, I thought. I had always felt very *un*photogenic, as I was self-conscious about my slightly uneven front teeth. To my great surprise the photos turned out well. "I didn't doubt for one moment that they would be beautiful," John said, "I don't know why you worry so much about your teeth, I don't see anything wrong with them."

We both departed Lisbon in December of 1951. John went back to the States and I went to Holland to get a visa. As an *immigration* visa would take years to obtain, John arranged with friends in the States to become my sponsors, enabling me to get a *visitor's* visa.

I left Holland on the *Westerdam* two months later, due to arrive in Hoboken, NJ on Monday, February 25. The closer I got to New York, the more excited I became. I was going to see John again! We were getting married!

John met me at the pier, in uniform, looking gorgeous. After lots of hugs and kisses we started our new adventure *together.*

In the two-year old Chevrolet John had just purchased we drove to Washington DC. Cars in the fifties had one long front seat, without a console in the middle. I sat snuggled up to John while he drove. During our first stop I wrote my parents:
We can't believe it yet that we're back together again. We're so elated and feel like millionaires in our new car.

John added a few words: *Hello, Mom, Pop and Family, am very happy to be able to tell you that our Paula (my "Duchess"), is now in good hands. You have nothing to worry about, so relax and help us to be completely happy by not worrying.*

Jim and Dorothy, the Air Force couple that had sponsored me, lived in Virginia. John had visited with them before my arrival and made all the arrangements to get married on March 1. When he called them Tuesday morning they told him, we *had* to be in Virginia the following day if we wanted to get married that Saturday.

Some frenzied shopping followed. Yes, in one afternoon we bought our plain gold wedding rings (mine cost $6, John's $9) and a suit for me with blouse, hat, shoes, handbag, and gloves. John was all set—he planned to wear his Dress Blues. It being a leap year, we had one much needed extra day to get a marriage license, blood tests, and order a cake and flowers.

On March 1, 1952, we were married in the chapel at Langley Air Force Base, with Jim and Dorothy as our witnesses.

After being forced in Portugal to wait so long for this moment John looked at me and said, "Mrs. Boswell, are you as happy as I am?" Thrilled to hear my new name I answered, "Honey, I'm the happiest girl in the world."

Shortly after we set out on our honeymoon, while driving through a one-horse town, we briefly came down to earth when a policeman signaled us to move over. John rolled down his window. "What can we do for you, officer?" he asked innocently. "Do you know you drove straight through a red light? Lucky for you there was no traffic." We apparently had been so wrapped up in each other that we had missed seeing the stoplight. Looking at John's Dress Blues and my outfit the policeman then asked, "Are you by chance newly-weds?" When he heard that we indeed had just gotten married he told us to continue on our trip but not without a warning to pay more attention to our surroundings.

In North Carolina we started to look for a motel. Fancy hotels were only found in the big cities in the fifties; on the road all you could find were simple motels. NO VACANCY, NO VACANCY, flashed the signs in town after town. After a lot more searching we finally found a place with a vacancy sign.

We spent our wedding night in a $4 motel room. To us, it felt like the Presidential Suite.

At a "fado" restaurant

January 1951: John and Paula got engaged in Holland

Formal portrait of Paula, age 26

At an American Embassy ball

The wedding on March 1, 1952 at Langley Air Force Base

Cutting the wedding cake

CHAPTER 20

Culture Shock

Three days into our honeymoon we arrived in John's hometown: *Bonifay, Florida.* John was nervous; he later told me he had been worried about how I would react to his family. Just before entering the small town he said, "Anytime you feel you want to leave, just tell me; I'll understand."

Though John had made me aware that most of his family had little money, the reality came as a culture shock to me. Many homes still had outhouses and pumps for drinking water. The insides were furnished with only the bare essentials with very few luxuries. Inevitably, I started to think about my family in Holland. My modest home in The Hague seemed like a royal palace compared to most homes in Bonifay.

I was glad John declined the many invitations to stay with family during our visit. We found a motel and spent almost a week in Bonifay. How did we fill our days? Simple—John had a lot of relatives. I had always wanted to be an "auntie." Here I was "Aint (southern for *aunt*) Paula" to at least six dozen nieces and nephews.

Not having lived in the South since the age of seventeen, only a few, though undeniable, traces of John's origins were detectable. (He did use lots of colorful southern *expressions* all his life.) But what the "natives" spoke sounded almost like a foreign language to me at first. Not only did they pronounce several vowels differently, but they swallowed whole syllables.

To make matters worse, many of his family members *mumbled.* I just sat there, staring at their barely-moving lips, hoping that I nodded or shook my head at the right moment when they looked my way.

I was never bored and fell from one surprise or funny situation into the next. There was a family (I have no clue how John was related—I quit keeping track after the first morning) with thirteen kids. Their first and middle initials went through all twenty-six letters of the alphabet. (I'm not making this up.) I don't remember their exact names of course, but it was something like: Albert Brutus, Cora Denise, Edward Franklin, you get the picture, all the way to Y-Z. Years later, we heard this oddity was written up in the Guinness Book of World Records! Talking about names, it was strange for me to hear John being called *Ray* and *Uncle Ray.*

Some of his relatives were characters. There was Holden, for example, one of John's much older half-brothers. He and his wife Edna actually had some nice pieces of furniture plus lots and lots of bookshelves filled with music rolls to use in a player piano. We didn't see a piano, so John got curious and asked about it. "Well, Ray," Holden said in answer to John's query, "we decided to sell it as we never played it anymore." "Didn't you sell the music rolls with it?" John wondered. "No, we wanted to keep the rolls just in case we'd change our mind and get another piano." I guess you could call that Bonifay logic.

One quality that struck me was the *southern hospitality,* which was so different from what I had been used to in Holland. Sure, when my mother *invited* people over she was a gracious hostess. But if one of us kids innocently brought a friend home with us close to dinnertime she had, what my Bonifay "sisters" would call a "hissy fit." I actually had to tell my friends *sorry, but you better go home.* Embarrassing! In Bonifay it was the total opposite. We were welcomed with open arms anywhere at any time of the day. If we happened to arrive around five, trying to squeeze in one more visit before dinner we were immediately invited to stay and have "supper" with them. And they wouldn't take *no* for an answer. In Bonifay they never said they were *glad* you came, it was always, "I'm so *proud* you came. I'll just take another chicken from the fridge; supper will be in just a little while. Here, have a glass of sweet tea and some boiled peanuts." Yes, *boiled peanuts.* Even in 2003, our last visit, there were street vendors selling boiled peanuts. John loved them. As for me, give me *roasted* peanuts any day. Dried "chitlings" (chitlins in southern speak) were another "treat" in Bonifay. They are crunchy and look like a small nut. People eat them by the handful. Don't let the looks deceive you; they are made from the intestines of a hog.

To get back to dinner: in less than an hour several pots full of steaming food were put on the table. "Dig in y'all," came the word. I'll try to describe my first meal in Bonifay. The biscuits were delicious. The southern fried chicken was good. There was another meat dish with lots of bones I thought I'd better leave alone. But then came the vegetables. Oh, gee, did I really have to eat those? Not wanting to offend our hostess I politely took a small spoonful from one pot. It looked like a slimy, stringy mess to me. "That's *okra*, honey, try some," John encouraged me, "and have some *taters.*" Another pot contained turnips and collard greens. For dessert we had "sweet-potato pie." John was in *hog heaven.*

How to describe John's mother? Not *sweet*, more like *feisty.* It was obvious she loved John, her youngest, with all her heart. She was thrilled John had found true happiness and pleased to meet his new bride. John always treated his mom with great love and respect.

Mom Boswell, *Florence* to most, never sat still. She was always *tendin' to* or *fixin' to do* something: preparing food for canning, pickling, and salting, or sweeping the floor. She also was an avid quilter; she was a member of a quilting bee, as were two of her sisters. The bee took place at the house of her sister Lydia, who had a big quilting frame, which she would pull down from the ceiling to work on a quilt and pull it up again after they were finished. For a wedding present Florence gave us two of her masterpieces.

Not all John's relatives were poor. He had a cousin *Plunk Boswell* in Alabama, who owned a huge, profitable farm with a beautiful lakeside home. They had sailboats and motorboats with water skis.

In Bonifay, disregarding the professionals like doctors, attorneys, bankers, and the like, most people didn't seem to *want* to improve their situation. Some of them even *resented* it when you tried to better yourself. I remember when we stopped by in '56, on our way to California. When John told Reedy, another half-sister, that he planned to go to college, she gave him the word: "Whatcha tryin' to do Ray, get above your raisin'?" To which John replied, "Reedy, I'm trying to get as far above my raising as I possibly can." That didn't mean he looked down on his family and origins; far from it, he loved all his relatives dearly. He just couldn't see getting stuck in a rut when there was something better out there. Reedy, *bless her heart,* had to eat crow years later. One of her own sons left at a young age for Texas, got a college degree and established himself as a dentist.

What pleased John in years to come was the fact that quite a few of his nieces and nephews—the younger generation—followed his example; they either went into the service, attended college, or found better employment outside Bonifay. John had shown them it co*uld be done.*

When we left Bonifay, resuming our honeymoon, John was beaming. "I know this wasn't easy for you, darling. I'm so proud of you and so thrilled you accepted my family for who they are. They all loved you." How could I *not* have liked these caring, charming, and funny people who were part of John's heritage?

There are a few more memorable stories about Bonifay I'll leave for another chapter.

CHAPTER 21

Mom Boswell and the Beast

While John was stationed in Shanghai, China, he met a Marine named Joe, who grew up within thirty miles from Bonifay. His parents sent him copies of the weekly local paper. One morning Joe was reading the paper when John happened to pass by. "Hey, Johnny, come look at this, any relations?" he laughed, handing John the paper. John looked at it, astonished at first, then letting out a *whoop:* "I can't believe it, that's my mother they are talking about." The headlines on the front page said something like this:

BONIFAY FARMER'S WIFE HAS SCARY EXPERIENCE

A few paragraphs followed with a brief description of what had happened to *Florence Boswell* some nights ago.

After Florence's death in 1967, John's cousin and boyhood friend Chuck Singletary wrote a tribute to her. It told in great detail about that "scary night." Here it is, in Chuck's words:

MY FAVORITE AUNT

Aunt Florence was my mother's oldest sister and the oldest of a family of thirteen. She had to assume adult responsibilities before she was old enough. When her mother became disabled at an early age, Aunt Florence did most of the household chores in addition to caring for her younger brothers and sisters. Consequently, she did not have much chance for an education, but she was blessed with an unusual amount of common sense. She also had a delightful sense of humor. She taught herself to read and write and became an avid reader. She married a much older widower with children almost her age.

Now comes the story:

One night, around two in the morning, she was awakened by a loud crashing noise that sounded as if the barn had exploded. She jumped out of bed without awakening her husband and ran out in her nightgown to see what all the noise was about. The moon was bright and what she saw almost gave her a heart attack. The whole side of the barn was caved in and, standing in the middle of the barn, eating corn, was the largest animal she had ever seen, almost as large as the barn! She ran into the house to wake my Uncle Ab and told him there was a monster in the barn and she was going for help and for him to stay put. They did not have a telephone.

The nearest neighbor lived almost two miles away. Aunt Florence threw a coat over her nightgown and grabbed her wide-brimmed hat she wore for protection from the Florida sun. Heading up the road in the pitch dark she was delayed several times along the way as her hat kept blowing off. Florence would never leave her hat, so each time it blew off she would stop, run back to get her hat, put it back on her head and continue running up the road to her neighbor's house.

Upon arrival she was so out of breath that she had difficulty trying to explain what had happened. When she finally got the words out the neighbor didn't believe her but, having a phone, called the sheriff anyway.

The sheriff came at once and took my aunt and her neighbor with him to investigate the situation. She took them to the barn where they saw...a jumbo-sized elephant! There were no zoos within a hundred miles, so they had no idea where the beast came from.

In the meantime, back in the sheriff's office, a message had come in reporting a lost elephant. No one was aware of the fact that a traveling circus had passed through the area. When the truck carrying the elephants had a flat tire, they unloaded the beasts in order to fix the flat. This particular elephant had wandered off in the dark without being detected until they started to re-load. By the time the report came in the elephant was three miles away, in the Boswell's corncrib. Since Florence had never seen an animal larger than a horse, one can imagine her fear when she was confronted with a jumbo-sized elephant.

John heard later that the circus crew paid for the repair of the barn plus the corn and hay the elephant had eaten. In the meantime, he had to endure a lot of ribbing from his buddies. "That's a helluvaway for your folks to get famous, Johnny!"

CHAPTER 22

The Ups and Downs of a Marine Wife

Shortly after getting back from our honeymoon John received orders for his next duty station: Camp Pendleton, CA.

Just before our cross-country drive to the West Coast I was quite sure I was pregnant. We were elated! At first I felt great. *"Pregnancy is a snap,"* I wrote my mom. Famous last words…. Soon morning sickness became all-day sickness. Driving through the Rockies with all its hairpin turns was pure agony.

The minute we arrived at our destination John took me to the Navy Hospital, hoping to get some relief for me. *They would not let me see a doctor.* A very uninterested nurse asked me upon arrival in a slow, nasal voice, "How many periods have you missed?" When she heard I had missed only two, she told me to come back after three. "Didn't you tell me that Navy Hospitals were so efficient?" I whined dejectedly. John, knowing how I felt, took me to a private doctor. Besides telling me I was two months pregnant, he gave me a lot of good advice and anti-nausea pills. Unfortunately, the pills didn't help—I was sick for over three months.

Our immediate concern now was to find a place to live, which brought more problems, as there was a severe housing shortage. We looked at available living quarters on the base. I was aghast! "Don't tell me people are actually *living* in those things," I said to John after seeing a bunch of *Quonset huts.* Yes, they did, I was told, both officers and enlisted men.

John could take a hint and intensified his efforts. Through an old friend we were able to get a tiny, one-bedroom, furnished apartment on a motor court in nearby Oceanside. However, it wasn't available until a month later. All we could find for the interim was a somewhat run-down studio apartment. At least we had a roof over our head.

During the first four weeks after our arrival I felt absolutely horrible. Camp Pendleton is a huge base, and John's office was thirty miles from the main gate. He left at 6:30 a.m. and returned at 6:00 p.m. During the day I felt terribly alone. There I was, in a new town in a strange country. I didn't have any friends or relatives anywhere near, and was too sick to go even for a walk. What did I get myself in to? I sometimes asked myself. To make matters worse, through some *snafu* at the base, no mail from Holland was delivered to John's military address for weeks.

John tried to cheer me up at night. Desperately wanting to do something for me to make me feel better he came up with an idea. "Why don't we settle in Holland after I retire in five years?" I brightened up immediately. "That's a fantastic idea, honey, but are you positive *you* want to do that?" He assured me he did, as long as it would make me happy.

I realized anew what a jewel of a man I had married. I wrote my mother:

> *John is an absolute angel. There are days I feel so rotten that I leave the house a mess with dishes in the sink and no dinner made. Instead of being annoyed at that when John comes home he is only unhappy that I feel so lousy. Even though he is tired after a long day's work he cleans up, does the dishes, and gets something to eat. I promised him, that as soon as I start feeling better, I'll cook him the best dinner ever.*

Slowly my nausea started to subside and my appetite returned. As I had lost five pounds since becoming pregnant I could now make up for it. But only to a point; the total weight-gain allowed while pregnant during the fifties was a maximum of twenty pounds. The doctors were very strict about that. The second time you gained more than two pounds between monthly visits they'd put you in the hospital on a buttermilk diet.

I should mention here that after I started to get my energy back, I returned to the Navy Hospital. Though John left that decision entirely up to me, I worried that in case of complications the cost of a private hospital could be astronomical.

When I was about five months pregnant and two weeks away from my next scheduled doctor's visit, a package arrived from Holland with lots of marzipan. As I had already gained my allotted two pounds I knew I absolutely *had* to stay away from sweets until after my weigh-in. Not to tempt my willpower I locked the marzipan in a box and gave John the key.

Immediately after my doctor's visit I rushed home. "Where's the key to the candy box?" were my first words on entering the house. John chuckled. "Darn, I forgot where I put it." Totally sweet-deprived and knowing that my favorite Dutch candy was just a few feet away, I shouted, "John, you can't do that to me. I'll get an axe and break the box down." He finally relented and I got my "fix." His reaction to my outburst and impatience was: "You know, this is the first time I've seen you behave like a typical pregnant woman."

Life improved greatly when we moved to the other apartment. The motor court consisted of twelve units, six on each side, with a lawn in the middle. We shared one very old, outmoded washing machine. You had to put your clothes through a wringer before hanging them out to dry. A freight train ran right behind our unit each morning around 5:00 a.m., whistling loudly.

Though not exactly an ideal situation, we had some wonderful times there with our neighbors, mostly young Marine

Corps couples like us. We shared everything, had parties on the lawn, and helped each other when we could. With the thought of settling in Holland John and I continued his Dutch lessons that we had started for fun in Lisbon.

Only one of us in the court had a phone. Its owner related messages to us from (often delayed) husbands. I became good friends with three other Marine wives. They teased me relentlessly about some of the expressions I used, translated straight from Dutch. Once I told them that the water in my sink did not *walk* out fast enough. Laughter. Another time I mentioned that my clock *stood still*. More laughter and remarks: "Oh, did your clock decide to take it easy for a while?"

Some of my neighbors seemed bemused by all my—unanswerable—questions. After finding only "Wonder Bread" in the supermarket I asked, "Where can I buy some *good* bread?" "What do you mean?" came the answer. "Well, isn't there a bakery in town that makes fresh, crunchy bread each day?" I wondered. I soon found out that the kind of bread I had eaten all my life was non-existent in the States (and wouldn't be available until many decades later).

The absence of decent bread wasn't the only matter that mystified me. With such a great climate and so much sunshine, why weren't there any outdoor cafés? And why did people take their car to go on an errand just around the corner? Why didn't anyone ride a bicycle? As there seemed to be no answers I decided to just enjoy all the pleasant aspects of living in America and forget about the few inconveniences.

Our favorite Sunday outing was a trip to Knott's Berry Farm with its famous chicken dinners and biscuits with boysenberry jelly. (Disneyland wasn't built yet.)

A few times during our stay in Oceanside we visited with Bill Pons, my mother's oldest brother, who had left Holland in his early twenties to seek a better life. He and his family lived north of Los Angeles, more than a three-hour drive from our place (before interstates). During one of those visits they took us out to dinner at the Brown Derby, a famous restaurant in

Hollywood, often filled with celebrities. We met Bob Hope, who seemed irritated when asked for his autograph, and very friendly Doris Day—our favorite singer! When I mentioned how we loved her songs she wanted to know all about us. She signed our menu, which unfortunately got lost over the years.

On Election Day all of us on the court sat around one TV, hoping for Eisenhower to get elected. We got our wish. John and I also started to watch "I love Lucy" at one of the neighbor's. We got so hooked on the show we decided to buy our own TV, a 17-inch black and white.

John often had to go on two and three-week long maneuvers, preparing the Marines for combat in Korea, a very scary thought. I remember our anxiety when one day an announcement was made in Camp Pendleton: "Because of heavy casualties in Korea, one thousand Marines are needed immediately for replacement." The men were to be chosen the next day from the division John and our neighbors belonged to.

The following morning I kissed John goodbye with fear in my heart that he would return with bad news. All of us wives stuck together that entire day, worried sick about what we might hear that night. John was the last of the men in the court to return.

"Honey, I'm not going anywhere," were his joyful words on coming through the front door. Though extremely relieved, I couldn't help thinking about the sadness a thousand other young families were experiencing that evening.

When I was eight months pregnant I received a letter from the U.S. Immigration Department: "You are hereby informed that your immigration papers will be ready to sign at the American Consulate in Tijuana, Mexico on November 20." According to an idiotic law in existence I had to physically *leave* the country as a visitor in order to *return* as a permanent immigrant.

Tijuana in the fifties was a typical Mexican border town, consisting of a few messy streets filled with shops selling leather goods, silver, and cheap souvenirs. The outer areas were mostly slums.

On the appointed day we drove the fifty-plus miles south to Tijuana. I was sweating it out. What if something went wrong? What if my papers weren't in order? The thought of having to deliver our baby in a Mexican hospital was frightful.

After a two-hour wait at the consulate I received my immigration visa. It was with intense relief that we crossed the border back into the United States. I was now a legal immigrant. It would take another five years before being eligible for citizenship.

For months I had been decorating a plain wicker bassinet for our baby-to-be. With the material and ribbon I bought it eventually turned into a work of art (in my humble opinion). My neighbors admired my work. "Gosh, you could make a fortune in New York City selling bassinets," they remarked. Then they added that it really was a waste of time, as the baby would outgrow it in a matter of months. I didn't care; I wanted our little baby to live in lavish surroundings for a while instead of being plunked at once into a big, cold crib.

On December 17, 1952, we became the proud parents of an adorable baby girl, Joyce Marilyn. Life seemed complete with one minor exception: my beautiful natural-curly hair had become totally straight. I never got a satisfactory answer when I asked my doctors what had caused that. "It's hard to tell; it may have been a side effect of the anesthesia," was the best they could come up with.

It didn't take long before we realized how little we knew about raising a baby. Dr. Spock's *Baby and Child Care* became our bible.

After Joyce was born we desperately needed a larger apartment. With all the extra furniture we could barely move about. So we put our name on a list of newly built three-bedroom rentals and hoped for the best.

In March, to our great delight, we got a call that one was available for us. Other than a stove and refrigerator, the house was *empty*. John took a few days leave; we left Joyce with friends, and went to San Diego to go *furniture shopping!* There were a lot of ex-Marines in business, eager to give their former buddies a good deal. In no time at all we bought, either on sale or second-hand, the basic stuff to furnish our house. To give it a European touch I insisted on a *round* coffee table. "That doesn't exist," we were told. After a long search I found one, though in unfinished wood.

Three days later all our purchases were delivered to our door. On my new sewing machine I made curtains, bedspreads, and slipcovers for the (second-hand) couch. We were in business! The grand total we spent on furnishings was $300. As soon as we were all settled in our new home, having a cup of tea together, we looked at each other and said with great contentment, "This is the life!!"

Joyce and her Daddy shortly before our separation

Three months later John came home with bad news: "I got my orders for Korea." I was devastated at first. However, as peace negotiations were in full swing there was still hope the war would end soon and his orders would be cancelled. Though a few days later a peace agreement was indeed signed, our jubilation over that joyful news was short-lived; John's whole division was sent to Japan as occupation forces. Within days all our treasured belongings were packed up. We tearfully kissed each other goodbye.

I spent the duration of John's overseas assignment with Joyce in Holland with my Dutch family. After just sixteen months of marriage we were separated for an entire year. Yes, that's the risk you take when you marry a service man. At that point I hated the Marine Corps. We were both looking forward to John's retirement in 1957.

CHAPTER 23

A Forced Separation

John left for Japan late in July of 1953 with the Third Marine Division. We were both terribly unhappy about this separation; John adored his little family and hated to have to miss an entire year of Joyce growing up.

Since we had heard that the Marine Corps often paid for dependents' trips home during a separation like ours, John put in a request before he left. My next concern was a passport for Joyce. Children too young to travel alone, under normal circumstances, are added to a parent's passport. However, when a mother and child are of different nationalities, that's not possible; eight-month old Joyce needed her own U.S. passport.

After waiting for over a month for word on military transportation, I was notified that the Marine Corps would only pay for the trip from Oceanside to wherever John was going to be stationed after his return. In other words, I was on my own. I immediately made plane reservations. The only way to fly from Los Angeles to Amsterdam was with a stopover in New York.

We arrived in New York at around 10:00 a.m. where I was informed that the KLM flight to Amsterdam had been delayed for at least three hours. The three hours turned into five, then seven. In those days the New York airport (I think it was La Guardia) was not air-conditioned. There I was with a tired, crying baby in a hot airport without even a place to heat up a bottle. I ran out of diapers and had to use disposables which were made of coarse paper—definitely not Pampers! When I reached the limit of my patience I set out to find someone who could help me. A supervisor took pity on me and let us stay in his office, one of the few air-conditioned rooms.

At long last my plane for Holland left. Joyce slept almost the entire flight over.

My Dutch family was elated to have us come for a whole year. Everyone was constantly playing with Joyce and talking to her. It's no wonder she started to talk when she was just one year old, whole sentence with many difficult words, in Dutch of course. Instead of calling my mother "Oma," she pronounced it "Aba." My dad became her "Opa."

We exchanged numerous letters and pictures during that year. John's letters to me were long, handwritten epistles, very sentimental at times and full of longing. Here are some excerpts: *I sure look forward to the day we are all settled in our own home. It will be more wonderful than words could express."*

From another letter: *I can hardly wait till we are all together again. WOW! What a time we're going to have. It's no fun to be separated from my bride, especially on the second year of an 85-year honeymoon!*

John was constantly buying presents for us. Lots of packages arrived with Japanese kimonos and jackets for both of us, dolls for Joyce, and jewelry for me. As I had heard that Noritaki dinnerware was inexpensive in Japan I asked John to send a brochure with patterns for me to choose from. Each time I mentioned the china he would write back, *I haven't had a chance yet to look for the dishes you want but I found....* What followed were the items he *did* buy, almost all jewelry and sterling objects. To my regret he never bought the Noritaki. The gifts I treasured most were a pearl necklace, sets of sterling teaspoons, and cocktail forks with intricate designs.

During our forced separation I began to see the U.S. in a whole new light. Though my family was wonderful to Joyce and me during that year, I realized Holland wasn't really as great as I had remembered. Except for the bread (!) the Dutch food I had been craving wasn't all that special after eating it a few times. The gloomy, often rainy weather for months on end became depressing. It didn't help either that it happened to be the coldest winter in over fifty years. I started to think about the ease of life in the States, the opportunities for anyone wanting to work hard. And after John's retirement we could choose an area to settle with wonderful weather. Not only did I want John back but his country as well.

At long last John's joyful news arrived that his division was expected to go back to the States in July. It wasn't easy to coincide my arrival in New York with his. Once John knew when our ship would arrive, his commanding officer came to the rescue, arranging for John to *fly* back (instead of going by ship like the rest of his division), so he could meet us on time.

Our ocean liner ran into a big storm; we were both seasick half the time during the eight-day crossing. After the storm abated I put Joyce in the ship's nursery, where she soon learned some English words.

John stood waiting for us at the bottom of the gangplank. What a reunion! John immediately wanted to hold Joyce and was crushed she at first didn't want anything to do with him—a total stranger to her. Fortunately it didn't take long before she became friendlier. Before the day was over she said "Daddy" to John's great delight. It was the end of July 1954. We were a family again.

When I mentioned to John I had decided against living in Holland after retirement he beamed: "That's what I hoped you'd tell me." He often said to friends, "Sending Paula to Holland for that year was the best investment I ever made."

Before leaving Oceanside a year earlier John had traded in his old Chevy for a new Pontiac, which we now picked up at the factory in Detroit. From there we drove to his new duty station: Parris Island Marine Recruit Depot in Beaufort, SC.

Apart on our 2nd wedding anniversary

John in front of Mt. Fuji, Japan. 1954

John looking at pictures of his wife and daughter

Saying goodbye to the Dutch family.
From left to right: Hans, Pop, Joyce, Toto, Paula, Mom

CHAPTER 24

The Worst Place on Earth

The birth of our son, nine months after our reunion, was by far the best thing that happened to us in Beaufort, SC. We named him Luke Asberry, a combination of the names of my older brother and John's father. We were elated to have both a son and daughter now—our family was complete!

Shortly after our arrival in Beaufort—for lack of a decent rental—we had *bought* a brand new house for a total price of $6500: $500 down and $75 per month. That was it, no closing cost or anything. I have no idea what kind of a sales contract we signed.

Our new home had three bedrooms—no complaint about that. Upon seeing the big back yard, John's immediate remark was, "Hey, I'm going to plant watermelons, my favorite fruit." Sure enough, six months later we had more watermelons than we knew what to do with. Our kids and grandchildren inherited John's love for watermelons. To his disappointment and disbelief—"how can you possibly *not* like that delicious fruit?"—I never developed a taste for it.

John had told me jokingly, that the Marine Corps, in order to test the endurance of new recruits, put its bases in the worst possible locations. As far as Parris Island was concerned, he was right!

With the arrival of warm weather I soon came to the conclusion that no place on earth could have a worse climate. The long Beaufort summers were stifling hot with humidity readings equaling the temperature. No cooling off during the night. If that wasn't bad enough, there were *gnats*, millions of them everywhere, pesky little black flying critters that landed on anything damp or strong-smelling. Window screens were of no use—gnats flew straight through them.

For one special occasion I cooked a turkey. It had been a very hot and humid day. We left all the screened windows open, hoping to catch at least a little breeze. I took the turkey from the oven, set it on the table and turned back to the stove to make gravy. Less than five minutes later I started to put the rest of the food on the table, ready to call the family to sit down. That's when I noticed that the turkey was literally black, completely covered with gnats that had come in through the screens. I lost it. Picking up the entire turkey and dumping it in the garbage I screamed at John, "The heck with saving money, I *want an air conditioner!!*"

Very few houses had AC at that time—it was still a novelty. John didn't need much convincing and bought a large window unit the next day. What a relief. We kept it on day and night. We not only slept much better but John's health improved with the wonderful cool air. His offices on Parris Island were not air-conditioned.

We did have some pleasant experiences mixed in with the bad. One day during April of 1956 John came home from the base, saying, "You never guess who came to see me today." He proceeded to tell me that just after he lectured a group of new recruits on the use of gas masks a big chauffeur-driven staff car pulled up. As the car came closer John noticed its license plate with three stars, indicating the presence of a three-star general.

Uh-oh, John thought, it's coming straight at me; this can't be good news. As soon as the car stopped, a rear window was rolled down and someone yelled, "John Boswell, get over here." A little bewildered, yet knowing he couldn't disobey a three-star general, John hurried over. He was astounded when he recognized the visitor: General Puller, his former executive officer, whom he had served as flag bearer in Shanghai. "John Boswell, glad to find you well," the general said, "I saw your name on a roster and thought I'd come by to see what you've been up to." They talked for about ten minutes.

John was perplexed and in awe that this legendary man, one of the Corps' most renowned heroes, had remembered him from fifteen years ago. Even more so, that he had taken the time to come to his office, out in the boonies, to see him.

Because of several drowning deaths during recent night maneuvers at Parris Island, the general had been called from retirement to help with the defense in the ensuing court case that made national headlines.

Needless to say, the other Marines who witnessed John's conversation with this famous general gained new respect for their "Top," as master sergeants are often called.

I found the above incident even more amazing when I recently discovered a clipping from a Marine Corps newspaper of April 1954, while John was stationed at Camp Gifu in Japan. For a column "Caught for a Quote," John was asked, "Who is your selection as the Marine Corps outstanding personality?" John answered, "Chesty Puller is my idea of a real field trooper and a great Marine."

* * *

I haven't mentioned yet that Joyce, after leaving Holland, learned to speak English in no time at all. For a long time she continued speaking Dutch to *me*, but English to everyone else. She was completely bilingual. A typical conversation whenever she had a little friend over would go like this: "Joyce, where are the doll clothes?" the friend asked. Joyce turned to me: "Mommie, waar zijn de poppekleertjes?" After I answered in Dutch she in turn told her friend, "They are in the pink box in the closet." This stopped abruptly when she was about three. She made the emphatic statement one day: "I don't want to talk like that anymore, nobody else does." From then on, no matter what I said or asked in Dutch the little rascal would answer, "I don't know what you're saying." When I repeated my request in English she would jump up to fulfill my wishes."

Many years later, when Joyce was fifteen, we took our children for a long visit to Holland during the summer. Immediately upon arrival she told all her relatives to speak only Dutch to her as she wanted to learn it again. Before our return she was able to keep up a conversation. Her first language had remained stored away in her brain.

In 1956, one year before retirement, John heard about a new perk for the Marines, a so-called "twilight cruise": on reaching eighteen years of service you were allowed to pick your final duty station.

After two years of heat and bugs we knew we would never want to settle in the South. We corresponded with Chambers of Commerce in several areas and came to the conclusion, that the San Francisco Bay Area was the very best place to live.

John put in a request and was granted a transfer to San Francisco. *SAN FRANCISCO!!* Life couldn't get any better. We were happy, had two wonderful, healthy children, and now were going to our dream city.

Joyce and her baby brother

The four Boswells, after Luke's baptism

CHAPTER 25

Paula's Gift Shop

During the two years we lived in Beaufort, John's job on the base was so far removed from its center that ride sharing was impossible. That meant I rarely had the use of the car. As Luke was a very good baby, while Joyce spent hours playing house with her dolls and stuffed animals, I had a lot of spare time. Sure, I had to do some cooking and cleaning (never my favorite pastimes), and occasionally sewed a dress for Joyce or me. I was fortunate enough to have a maid once a week, Mildred, who cleaned the entire house, did the laundry, and ironed. The going rate for such help was $3 *for the entire eight-hour workday.* She was also very good with the children.

I had been wondering what else I could do during the many hours while John was at work when I noticed the following ad in the paper:

Would you like to make extra spending-money? Sell our unique Christmas cards to friends and neighbors. Guaranteed results.

Hmm, maybe I can do that on the days Mildred is here, I thought. I sent out for a sample package and in no time took dozens of orders. Next, I tried their boxes of *every day greeting cards* with the same result. The card company also sold inexpensive but clever gift items, which I added to my "line." I enticed customers with a free gift for every new customer they referred to me. So far my *clientele* all lived within walking distance.

Several women asked if I could import some items from Holland, like (imitation) Delft Blue, small wooden shoes, and other European items unavailable in South Carolina. My mother became my Dutch supplier, sending packages almost every week loaded with cute knick-knacks and gift items from Holland. Not wanting to lug all the stuff with me I displayed them in our spare bedroom, sent out flyers and put a small ad in the local paper.

John built tables and shelves out of surplus wood from the base. Next he had one of his talented men paint a sign and voilá, I was in business: "Paula's Gift Shop." As I knew I had to collect sales tax, I obtained a resale license. Now I could stay home and have customers come to *me*. My "showroom" still looked somewhat barren, so I scouted around the house and found items we had bought or received as gifts in Europe and never used, like ashtrays, embroidered tablecloths, spoons, etc. Soon they were all for sale. John grinned when he saw some of his belongings displayed. "I'd better start locking my stuff away," he teased.

Also for sale were some of Joyce's unused toys and baby plates that still looked like new. One day she walked in while I had a customer. "Oh look!" she yelled out, "there's my plate and my...." Before she could finish I shooed her from the room.

My grandmother once sent me a cotton biscuit holder, which she had sewn herself. It was cleverly made, yet very simple. I bought some remnants in town and started sewing. They were so well received I soon made dozens at a time—*mass production.* They sold especially well inside a basket. Dozens of lightweight, very inexpensive baskets arrived from overseas. I also sewed aprons, baby booties, specialty Christmas stockings, anything unavailable in our small town.

In case you mistakenly think I had a booming business going, I was *thrilled* when I sold for $20 a day. There were days nobody showed up. But I was having fun and yes, making plans for a *real* gift shop after John's retirement.

On one of Mildred's workdays I had to make a quick run into town to buy material. A neighbor gave me a ride. I was gone less than an hour. On my return Mildred mentioned that two women, Marine wives, had come to the shop to browse. Mildred had called my good friend from next door (yes, we had a phone—$3 per month) who quickly came and waited on them. While Mildred was on the phone the two women had been *alone in the shop*.

After my return I looked around and immediately noticed a small stuffed bunny missing. I quickly checked my entire inventory. I knew exactly what I had in stock, each and every piece. Seven items were missing for a total of $18. A robbery! I called the police. Although they came and wrote it up, they didn't seem the least bit interested in such a very small theft.

As soon as John came home we started talking with our (involved) neighbor. Did she hear a name or perhaps see the car they were driving? Suddenly she remembered: "One of the girls mentioned she knew Paula from the Navy Hospital waiting room. She told me her baby was born the day after Luke's birth."

That's all John needed to know. The next day he checked with the hospital and discovered only one baby had been born on April 26. He found the father's name and rank (a buck sergeant) and set out to find him on the base. The man was completely taken aback and immediately admitted that yes, his wife had brought several gift items home.

He asked, "How in the world did you know it was my wife?" John replied that he had an elaborate anti-theft system in the shop and summoned him to come to our house that evening, with his wife and her friend.

They arrived at seven. "We are so sorry, we didn't mean to do it, I don't know what got into us," they half cried, and told us they already had gone to their priest to confess. They had the stolen merchandise with them. "No," I said, only too glad to make a sale, "I don't want stolen merchandise back. You can pay me for what you took or else I'll turn you in." Naturally, they paid.

We never heard from the police. John bragged, "From now on you can call me *Sherlock.*"

Paula's Gift Shop

Inside the shop

CHAPTER 26

The Chandelier

During our one year separation the Marine Corps put our household effects in storage. As soon as we moved into our new home in Beaufort all those crates and boxes were delivered back to us. John took a day off to help with the unpacking.

We tore open the first big box, anxious to find what was inside, excited to see our favorite belongings back. Instead we groaned, "Oh no, not *that* thing again!" It was our most hated possession, the one item we had hoped would get lost or stolen during transportation: *the chandelier!*

There is, of course, a story behind this most impractical acquisition. After leaving Lisbon in December of 1951, I spent two months in Holland, at home with my parents, waiting for a visa to the U.S. My mother, an avid shopper, took me to many sales, urging me to buy things I might need in my future home. I had no idea what an average home looked like in the States but figured it couldn't be that much different from Holland.

Little did I know! In Holland, older homes have high ceilings with an overhead chandelier in almost every room. So when I saw a gorgeous wrought-iron chandelier at an after-Christmas sale I didn't hesitate buying it.

When I wrote John about how many trunks I was going to bring with me on the ship to New York he worried that the immigration authorities would get suspicious about my being on a "visitor" visa. "They're never going to believe you're just coming to visit friends when they see all that stuff you're bringing for daily living. They may refuse to let you come ashore," he worried. So he arranged with an embassy Marine friend in The Hague, who was about ready to return to Washington, to have my things shipped over together with his.

Though I had told John about the chandelier, my "terrific find," he was in shock when—what he called—the monstrosity finally arrived. "It would look great in the Waldorf Astoria," he joked.

Storing it took half the space in our one and only closet in Oceanside. That chandelier was, undoubtedly, the last thing we needed in our home. Even when we moved to a larger house, it remained a nuisance.

During John's one-year stay in Japan I wrote him about the shopping my mom and I had done during the after-Christmas sales. He answered: *I'm so glad to hear you had a good time shopping with your mother. Even happier you didn't buy another chandelier!*

Miracles do happen! On one of our trips from Beaufort to John's family in Florida—a little over three hundred miles— we visited with William, one of John's half-brothers. He had bought the oldest house in Pensacola, a large mansion he planned to make into a combination museum and antique shop. He furnished it with items bought at auctions and estate sales. While admiring what he had accomplished so far, I noticed that in one large room, hanging from the ceiling, was a chandelier somewhat similar to our detested closet occupier. I pointed to it hesitatingly and said, "Hey William, would you be interested in another chandelier? I bought one in Holland." Imagine my surprise when he got very excited. "I've been looking all over for a second one. Bring it with you the next time you visit. In the meantime, look around and see if there's anything you may want to trade for it."

I couldn't believe my good luck. I already was drooling over a beautiful antique cedar chest in one of the rooms. "What about that cedar chest?" I asked with trepidation, afraid he would tell me that such an antique was worth much more than a wrought-iron chandelier. To my intense surprise and joy he answered, "If that's what you want for it, that's okay by me. I'll keep it for you."

A few months later we made the five-hour trip again. As the chandelier was too big for the trunk, the children had to share the back seat with it. With Luke in a car bed, it left very little room for Joyce.

To my great delight William enthusiastically made the trade. They had to unscrew the four-inch legs to fit the chest in the trunk. Frankly, I liked it better without the legs anyway, so we never put them back on.

The chest became one of our prized possessions, always taking up a prominent spot in our homes.

CHAPTER 27

Diamonds

Occasionally, during the first four years of marriage, I thought about my decision in Lisbon to forego a diamond engagement ring. Though diamonds in Portugal were far less expensive than in the U.S. I had found it so "un-Dutch." In Holland at that time, upon getting engaged, a girl was given a plain gold ring by her future husband to put on the ring finger of her *left* hand. During the wedding ceremony that same ring was then placed on her *right* hand. In my thinking, a diamond ring didn't signify "being engaged." I felt we could use the money better for more practical things, like a sewing machine once we were married.

I changed my mind not long after coming to the States, wishing I had not been so foolish in Portugal. Every wife I knew had a diamond ring. If I had insisted, I'm sure John would have bought me one. Yet, neither of us wanted to touch our savings.

We did start looking at rings though, in the jewelry department at—where else?—the Post Exchange on Parris Island. There was a lovely quarter-carat diamond ring on display for $53. We looked at it each time we shopped there. "As soon as we have some extra money I'll get it for you," John promised.

In May of 1956 John cashed in thirty days of leave. The Marine Corps allowed only sixty days of leave—accumulated over two years—to stay on the books. There comes my ring, I thought. However, John's mother had been begging us to come and visit, so she could see her new grandson. Besides, John was anxious to show off his children. So off to Florida we went. It took all the extra money. *No ring.*

In October of that year, shortly after John received his orders for San Francisco, we sold our house with a cash profit of $1300.

After the buyer left we jumped up and down from pure excitement for several minutes. Then John said, "Get your coat, we're going to the PX." We quickly put the kids in the car and set out, at long last, to buy my ring.

I was ecstatic. We found one ring exactly my size. John slipped it on my finger with the promise: "This is only the beginning. If we ever have plenty of money I'm going to buy you the most beautiful jewelry ever."

Joyce, not quite four years old, observed the whole procedure with great interest. "What kind of ring is that, Mommy?" she asked. I told her it was an engagement ring. John, always the joker, piped up, "Yes, your mother and I are getting married." Much later, when Luke started to talk, he put in his two cents' worth on the subject by asking, "Did you get that ring in a gumball machine?"

Though in later years we could have afforded a larger diamond, I always treasured my quarter-carat. We did have it put in another setting, surrounded by smaller diamonds.

Over the years, whenever the occasion arose, John kept his promise about buying me jewelry. Once in the nineties, we were in the wholesale jewelry department of the San Francisco Gift Center, looking for a Marine Corps ring. On the counter in one of the stores I noticed an absolutely gorgeous gold and diamond necklace, displayed on a large black velvet cushion. I casually said, "Isn't that the most beautiful necklace you ever saw?" It had a $10,000 price tag on it. The salesman quickly told us that the wholesale price was "only" $4000. "Let me buy it for you," John said. "Heavens no, that's way too much money," I gasped, "I don't need anything that expensive and extravagant." John kept on insisting: "Oh, come on, honey, I'd love for you to have that necklace, it'll look great on you." Then he turned to the salesman, handed him a credit card and said, "Go ahead, wrap it up for me."

What could I do with a man like that, other than give him a big hug? Not long after, we were able to buy him a solid gold Marine Corps ring through a mail-order catalog.

CHAPTER 28

San Francisco Here We Come

John's new—and last—assignment before retirement was at Headquarters, Dept. of the Pacific in downtown San Francisco (aka "the City"). We arrived in November 1956.

Our first concern was to find a place to live. Though rental houses were extremely scarce and apartments non-existent, there was an abundance of new homes for sale. As we had friends in Pleasant Hill, about a forty-five minute drive from the City, we decided to go house hunting in that vicinity.

Ever since my fledgling steps into the business world in South Carolina it had been my dream to find a *house and gift shop combination*. It was a European concept: using the basement or first floor as a shop and living in the rest of the house. Not long after we started our search I realized that such an arrangement was completely unattainable in the Bay Area. We shelved that idea right away.

In one housing tract the builders had just offered the model home for sale. A typical post-war house: three bedrooms, two baths, about 1200 square feet, with an already landscaped front and back yard. Being the model home, all drapes and curtains were included. It was ready for us to move in. The price was right and we were desperate, so we signed the papers and moved in less than ten days after arrival.

155

I'll never forget my very first trip to San Francisco. John had taken a day off to show me the wonders of our new surroundings. He explained the Caldecott tunnel, how it was built in 1937 to finally connect the Bay Area with the "hinterlands," resulting in the post-war housing boom. When we were almost at the west end of the tunnel he said, "Close your eyes for a few seconds." When he told me to open them again, there, in front of me, lay the most incredible panoramic view of the entire Bay Area. Houses hanging from the Berkeley and Oakland hillside. Far in the distance, yet clearly visible, were the Bay Bridge and the Golden Gate, with San Francisco and the Bay between them. I instantly fell in love and knew this was the place where I wanted to spend the rest of my life.

As we drove over the Bay Bridge more surprises came my way: Alcatraz, lots of little sailboats, and the enchanting skyline. It was unlike any other big city I had ever seen. And above all...what smells so wonderful? The aroma of freshly ground coffee wafted towards us, coming from roasting facilities close to the bridge.

Over the years we explored many more parts of San Francisco. Built on so many hills it reminded us of Lisbon. We also discovered Sausalito, Tiburon, Mt. Tamalpais, and other exciting places. We loved showing visiting relatives and friends our favorite sights.

We were not as thrilled with our new neighborhood. Though we liked the house, quite a few homes just around the corner were poorly kept. It taught us a lesson—look at the entire area first before buying.

The children had fun, though. As there was no through-traffic they could ride their bikes and play on the street with little danger. Often they went hunting for pollywogs with their new friends in the creek behind our house.

Five years later we "stepped up"—as the saying goes— to a bigger house in a new housing tract in Concord, about five miles away. As the completion date was months away we had plenty of time to sell our house in Pleasant Hill.

I remember when prospective buyers knocked on the door after seeing our *For Sale by Owner* sign. Saying I was not a terrific housekeeper is an understatement. John often teased me that I had married him *under false pretenses*. As a child he had read a book about life in a Dutch town: "Hans Brinker and the Silver Skates." It tells about Dutch housewives who are constantly scrubbing their floors and porches. "What happened to you?" he joked. I told him I had other talents. However, when your house is on the market it has to be in great shape. I managed, with pain, to keep it clean and clutter-free at all times. Prospective buyers invariably remarked to John that his wife was such an "immaculate housekeeper." John would just chuckle and without much conviction say, "Yeah, sure."

As soon as the sale was final the Dutch housewife resigned and I re-appeared. John was happy for another reason: "I'm so glad I can leave the toilet seat up again."

When we moved to our new home in the fall of '61, we at first decided to make only the essential improvements, like a fence and a lawn, reasoning that the house was just a step up towards our eventual dream home.

The moment we had spoken those words we looked at each other and said, "What are we doing?" What followed was a serious discussion about our life. We realized we were always chasing another dream, constantly thinking about and working towards new goals, towards a new phase, something bigger and better, *without fully realizing and appreciating the present.*

We came to the conclusion that it's all right to have goals as long as we didn't neglect the *here and now.* Too soon the children would be grown. The saying: "Dream as if you'll live forever, live as if you'll die today," took on new meaning.

CHAPTER 29

A Dream Fulfilled

When I first met John he came across as a very intelligent man. He could hold his own on just about any subject. So I was flabbergasted when he told me he only had a tenth grade education, dropping out of high school in his junior year. "Where did you get all that knowledge?" I asked him. That's when he told me he read a lot, mostly non-fiction books and magazines, not only on anything happening in the world now but also on history.

In 1953, while stationed in Japan, one of the first things he wrote me about was a trip to Osaka: *I bought a reading lamp with extension cord, which gives me a better chance to do more reading in the evenings. Just finished a book "The Iron Mistress," based on early American history.*

After his transfer to the Marine Recruit Depot in Parris Island, SC in 1954, John was lucky enough to get the job as the man in charge of "Elliott's Beach." He led new recruits through gas chamber drills and gave lectures on atomic warfare. As long as he did his job he could do whatever he wanted in the many hours left during the day. According to insiders it was the best job on the entire base for a master sergeant.

Wanting to make the best use of all that free time he requested a catalog with correspondence courses from the Marine Corps Institute. His first selection was a course in *Basic Electricity.* He finished that with good results in about three months. Next came a course in *Radio* and after that, *Television*. These culminated in day-long exams, supervised by one of his commanding officers.

The day after he took his final for *Radio,* he told me he had exams each day for the rest of the week. "Aren't these exams just for one day only?" I asked him. That's when he confessed he had been studying to take the high school equivalency test. Each day he had to take exams in a different high school subject.

He was thrilled to get his high school diploma at long last. That's when he started to talk about what he really wanted to do after retiring from the Marine Corps in 1957: go to college under the GI bill.

At age 37, just days after finishing his twenty years in the Marine Corps, he enrolled as a full time student in *Industrial Electronics* at Diablo Valley College, a community college in Pleasant Hill, CA, a fifteen minute walk from the house we had purchased. It would take him two years to get his AA degree.

This was not an easy study for him; he had to take classes in math and in subsequent semesters trigonometry, physics, and chemistry. I could help him with algebra but the other subjects were foreign to me. His grades were just average in those subjects. However, in required *communication* classes he excelled. I typed out most of his papers after he wrote them in the rough. When they were returned they always had remarks from the professor, like *excellent work* or *a pleasure to read.* This started us thinking that perhaps *electronics,* with all its science requirements, was not the right field of study for him.

During the summer of 1958, after his first year of college, he found a six-week job as director of a YMCA day camp for children from six to twelve years old. After his first day on the job John returned home beaming: "This isn't work, it's more like a paid vacation. I *love* working with these young children."

Over the next six weeks his enthusiasm didn't diminish. When the job ended John was sure that working with children was his true calling. "I never felt altogether comfortable with electronics, working with *things*," he confessed. Seeing how happy the summer job had made him I wholeheartedly agreed.

The decision was made; he was going to change his major to education and become a teacher. It was a good choice for another reason; there was an enormous shortage of teachers everywhere. As he had already completed half of the two-year electronics study he decided to finish the final year before switching over.

In June of 1959 he received his AA degree and in the winter of '60 transferred to the newly opened Cal State Hayward to become a teacher for grades K-8. He was in only the second graduating class, consisting of less than one hundred students. The professors and students all knew each other.

During his last year in college he did several stints as *student teacher*. He enjoyed it tremendously and knew he had made the right choice—he had found his niche.

When the first trimester of student teaching was over, the class he taught begged the principal: "Please make Mr. Boswell a teacher at this school." His supervisor later asked him what on earth he had been doing with those children, as the reports were so outstanding.

John finished his studies in March of 1962. Soon after, my mother wrote him a letter with congratulations. Typical of John, he didn't want to take all the credit himself for his accomplishments. He wrote her back:

> *It was so very nice of you to write me a letter of congratulations. Your thoughtfulness is certainly appreciated. I shall remember your kind words. You will understand how happy Paula and I are to share with you the joyful occasion that has at long last arrived.*
>
> *Let me hasten to point out, Mom, that whatever success I have gained has been a cooperative effort. I mean by that that I have not done this alone. Paula and I have done this together. We have worked as a team, and my wonderful wife deserves equal credit. Paula has*

worked to help support the family; she has been a constant source of support and encouragement in my academic efforts. Without Paula, this would not have been accomplished.

John had to wait till June for the actual graduation ceremonies. Joyce, Luke and I were all there to cheer him on. I had my camera ready, loaded with film. The ceremony was inside. Together with his fellow graduates John came walking down the aisle in cap and gown and then...the flash didn't work! I could just cry. I did take pictures outside to remember this milestone. While there, several of John's professors stopped by to congratulate him. They were full of praise for John and said to me, "Your husband should continue for a Master's Degree."

That's the last thing John wanted to do. He was so happy to be able to support his family again and enjoy life to the fullest without always having his nose in a textbook.

John and family after graduation in June 1962

CHAPTER 30

Camping

In the early sixties we befriended a family with kids about the same age as ours. Each time we got together they extolled the virtues of camping in the Redwoods; how wonderful it was for the children, how much fun they all had, and how beautiful the campgrounds were with hot showers and other amenities.

Both Joyce and Luke got very excited listening to all the stories about mountain trails, bubbling creeks with lots of trout to catch, sleeping in a tent, swimming in the river, and cooking meals on a little BBQ. They had no trouble convincing John. To get *me* to agree to a camping trip was another matter. In my mind I saw swarms of stinging mosquitoes and colonies of ants invading our food supply. NO WAY, I thought. The kids wouldn't give up: "Please, Mommy, please say yes, we promise we'll be the best children in the world."

Our friends offered to lend us all their camping gear so we could try the experiment without having anything to buy. John joined the children in their pleas: "Why don't we try it just once to see what it's all about. If you don't like it I swear I won't ever ask you again." I finally, reluctantly, relented. "Okay, I'll try but don't get your hopes up I'm going to like it."

Off we went to the Redwoods, leaving home around noon in our station wagon loaded with a tent, sleeping bags, air mattresses, a frying pan, food, and a few other necessities.

In the sixties, State Parks did not take reservations—it was strictly first come first served. We had a map with possible campsites. During the trip north John started to sing some of the many songs in his repertoire. Soon we all chimed in: "I've got sixpence, jolly jolly sixpence, I've got sixpence to last me all my life" and on and on. We had a ball. I started thinking, hmm, this is fun, it might not be so bad after all.

In less than three hours we reached the first redwood park. "Sorry, we're full." We tried another camp and got the same message. The kids were very disappointed. "We should have left much earlier," they lamented. After three more tries with negative results I was beginning to picture a nice motel with clean beds, a warm swimming pool, and dinner in a restaurant. As I was always the navigator on our car trips, John turned to me: "Aren't there any more parks on your map?" I would have loved to say NO, but in all fairness to the family I searched and searched and found a small redwood park, called *Grizzly Creek*, a little off the beaten track, seventeen miles into the boonies to be exact. It was decided if that one was full we would give up and find a motel.

You guessed it: *There was room!* By the time we paid our one-dollar entrance fee, it was early evening. It didn't take us long to find a vacant site close to the (immaculate) showers and bathrooms. The site was huge and right in the midst of towering trees. Joyce and Luke were elated: "Look, we've got our own little cupboard and a table and benches!"

They all helped setting up the tent and installed the sleeping bags. After a quick bite we set out to explore the park. I had to admit it was absolutely gorgeous. For a while we followed a trail, and then suddenly a vista opened up right before our eyes. It truly was like a living painting: the river, sparkling with the last rays of sunshine, slowly moving over countless rocks. Lush wooded hills rising from the riverbanks. Not a soul in sight. Except for the chirping of the birds there was total silence. The wonderful aroma of the redwood trees wafted over us. We all just stood there, in awe, unable to speak at first. It's hard to describe but I suddenly felt totally at peace. I wondered, is this what it means to feel close to God?

We took off our shoes and socks and started wading in the shallow part of the river, trying to hold on to the magic. Almost with reluctance we returned to our campsite to get ready for the night. Here a new experience awaited us: Pumping up the air mattresses. Swoosh, swoosh, swoosh, it was a lot of work! (Inflators operated by plugging them in to the car's cigarette lighter hadn't been invented yet.)

The next morning John said from the bottom of his heart, "That was the best night sleep I've had in a long, long time." We made a fire in the BBQ pit. John cooked breakfast: bacon, eggs, and pancakes—a real feast!

After breakfast we went on a hike, along the many nature trails. I only had to look at the kids' faces to know they were enjoying every minute of it. They quickly found friends their age and went exploring. While at home we had a hard time getting Luke out of bed in the morning, here he was up and going as soon as it was light, standing patiently by the water's edge, hoping to catch a fish with a make-shift rod. His first fish made him one happy little guy. We fried it for breakfast.

I started thinking about what I had feared. Where were the ants? I hadn't seen a mosquito yet. This wasn't all that bad. In fact, I admitted with some trepidation, it was actually wonderful. Would I do it again? In a heartbeat!

The day after we got home we went shopping. In short order we bought a tent and other necessary equipment, with the exception of a lantern, which we obtained by trading one book of Green Stamps—remember those? For many years we went camping several times each summer, discovering other redwood parks, camping at Crater Lake in Oregon, and on the shores of Lake Tahoe. Jedediah Smith Park, close to the Oregon border, was one of our favorites. Every night there was a big campfire with sing-alongs and a program on some aspect of nature with interesting, and amusing talks by the forest rangers.

Once we went on an overnight church camp-out. I should explain to the uninitiated that usually a sleeping bag has its own storage sac with attached cord for tying. When I woke up in the middle of the night I quickly glanced around. There was John, fast asleep. Joyce, ditto. Then, *panic!* Luke's sleeping bag looked empty. I screamed, tore the bag open and saw Luke *with the cord around his neck.* John, now wide awake, quickly evaluated the situation, jumped on top of his son and started artificial respiration. "What's the matter?" came Luke's sleepy, grouchy voice. They were the most wonderful words we had ever heard him utter. The cord was not really tied around his neck—it just looked that way.

In 1971 my brother Hans, his wife, and two children came over from Holland for a three-week visit. During their stay a trip to Yosemite was discussed. After listening to all our camping stories the kids wanted to try sleeping in a tent, a novelty to them. Our teenagers had other things to do, so there were six of us. Campsites in Yosemite weren't anything like in the Redwoods; they are close together with people all around you. As it would be too crowded in the tent for four adults and two children, John slept in the station wagon.

We had heard that bears roam around at night, looking for food. "Don't put your icebox on the ground," was the advice. So we put ours on the picnic table. In the middle of the night we heard a commotion. Peeking out of the tent we saw a bear demolishing our icebox, eating our food. Hans panicked. He ran to the wagon and shouted anxiously, "John, John, come quick, there's a bear, a *bear!*" John had already heard the noise and knew exactly what was happening. He got tickled and at first didn't answer, waiting to see what Hans would do. Hans ran back to the tent, grabbed a tent pole to defend himself, and yelled at the bear, "Ksh, ksh!" By that time John came to the rescue, making a lot of noise, banging pans. The bear finally ambled off.

For Hans and his family, who had never seen anything like this, it was a frightful experience. Later however, the story about Hans and the bear became a favorite topic of conversation. We also learned that "don't put your icebox on the ground" really meant you had to raise it *up* into the trees, high enough so a bear couldn't get to it.

CHAPTER 31

Wanna Buy A House?

Not long after John started to attend Diablo Valley College in the fall of '57, he brought home a catalog with class listings for the following semester. "Maybe *you* would like to take a class," he suggested.

Without much enthusiasm I flipped through its pages. Suddenly the title *Real Estate License Preparation* leaped out at me. Hmm, I thought, that might be fun. Maybe I could sell a house or two to ease our precarious financial situation.

It wasn't easy making ends meet on John's Marine Corps retirement plus the money from the GI bill, a grand total of $320 per month. To supplement our income I had started to baby-sit two neighbor children during the day. The idea of selling real estate appealed to me. I signed up for the class and started late in January: one evening a week from 7 to 10.

I truly enjoyed the course. The teacher, a real estate broker, encouraged me to take the exam. To make a long story short, I passed the exam and got a job close to home, working for a broker two or three evenings a week and on weekends. (Real estate offices were open until 9 p.m. during the summer in those days.) John took care of our children while I worked.

"Working" meant sitting in an office, hoping for prospective buyers to drop in or call on the phone. When people walked in I would first talk to them to find out what kind of a home they were looking for. Next I had to establish what monthly payments they could qualify for. Not until those preliminaries were out of the way would I begin showing houses.

I did my homework; in my free time I looked at all the houses for sale through the multiple listing system in a radius of about ten miles from our office, familiarizing myself with details and special features. It sped up the process, as it enabled me to match my buyers with ideal houses without having to show a lot of unsuitable ones. Often they made their choice after seeing just three or four houses. Once the decision was made, I took them back to the office, wrote up the *offer to buy* and was given a deposit. All that remained was acceptance from the seller. As few people offered full price, we often had counter-offers or had to take part of our commission on a note.

I should mention that most houses then sold for between $10,000 and $20,000. Often less than $1,000 was needed for down payment and closing cost. With the ease of buying and selling, a lot of people didn't stay long in one house, *moving up* after four or five years.

As soon as I began this new venture, John and I started dreaming about what we would buy if I sold a few houses. "One house, we'll buy a dishwasher, two houses the kids get new bikes, three houses and we might be able to get a piano."

Within the first five weeks I sold *four* houses. We were totally bowled over. As soon as I received my first check the dishwasher became a reality. I wrote my mother:
The sloshing water in the dishwasher, doing the work I detest, sounds like a symphony to my ears. A month later Joyce and Luke got their bikes, and we bought John a better guitar. Though John couldn't carry a tune, he sang enthusiastically with our children, his students, and much later the grandchildren, accompanied by his guitar playing.

I wrote my mom: *It's so nice not to have to turn over every penny, to be able to get groceries in just one store instead of going to five different ones to get their specials.*

I was particularly happy for John, who could now spend all his energy on his studies rather than worry about money. "If you keep on doing this well we'll invite your parents to come over next winter," he suggested. Three months later we bought a very good second-hand piano and in the winter of 1959 my parents visited.

Nobody eluded my zeal; I sold a house to the Avon Lady who came calling, and to the plumber who installed my new dishwasher. At times, when I had trouble getting a loan approved for a client, John came to the rescue with his writing skills. He wrote such convincing letters, both to private lenders and the FHA (Federal Housing Administration) that initial refusals were reversed.

For several years sales kept coming. One week I sold four houses in four days. Another time I met an elderly couple looking for houses as investment. I sold them five houses in quick succession. A year later they got tired of running after their tenants and asked me to *sell* them again.

We took the kids to Disneyland and got a new car. Often we went to San Francisco for dinner and a show. We both loved musicals. These outings to the City necessitated a new wardrobe for me. John got into the act and bought me a Russian squirrel stole. With all this dressing up I decided to wear a little more make-up. Big mistake! The first time I applied blue eye shadow John looked at me and asked, "Did you get hit in the eye? You are all black and blue." Another time, getting ready for a Christmas party, I wore a rhinestone tiara with matching necklace and earrings. For extra glamour I put silver glitter in my hair. John looked at it critically. "It looks as if you stood under a Christmas tree and someone shook it." Yes, John liked my natural look. I toned my make-up way down.

We bought two houses for investment, taking over the sellers' low interest loans and started to make plans to go to Europe in the summer of 1961. And of course we put money in savings. After several more exams I became a broker, which enabled me to open my own office if I so desired.

Then suddenly: *nothing!* Sales I wrote up fell through, buyers could not qualify or were unexpectedly transferred. After about four months with similar results I started to look for another job. A department store in the area offered me $1.25 per hour (minimum wage). But then I thought, just getting *one* listing commission would earn me more than working *one hundred hours* in retail. So I tried harder and did make a few sales. Previous clients called back with listings. Somehow though, my enthusiasm had waned. John would soon be graduating, meaning that I didn't *have* to work. The children loved it when I was home in the evening and on weekends.

I told my boss I was quitting. "You're crazy," he told me, "You were one of the best salesmen I ever had." I thanked him politely and went home.

Three months later I became a student at the local community college.

Dressed up for a fancy Christmas party

CHAPTER 32

My Father,
Paul van Dalsum

Paul van Dalsum, nicknamed Pol or Polly, came from an old aristocratic family. Though his father was a college graduate with a degree in mechanical engineering, he made his son quit high school when he was sixteen years old. Paul was to become part of the thriving family business selling butcher shop equipment.

In his twenties "Polly van Dalsum" was well-known in soccer circles. He was an outstanding player, often selected to play for the Dutch national team against other countries.

When we were growing up, Pop—Poppy when we were little—was a good father. He was a hard worker, trying to provide for his family, while spending little on himself. Yes, he was strict; we better not disobey his rules, or a spanking was waiting for us.

Sundays were almost entirely devoted to us. He took us on long hikes, along the beach or through the dunes. The highlight of such an outing was a visit to a restaurant for a glass of a syrupy fruit drink. Later in the afternoon we played card games with the whole family. As a special treat he sometimes baked waffles in a stovetop waffle iron. We ate those with butter and powdered sugar. They were delicious!

He made many critical decisions that proved beneficial to our family, like selling the house in Scheveningen and in particular, moving to the countryside after the Normandy invasion. During that last year of the war he tirelessly faced wind and rain to get us food.

Shortly after the war ended he became downright ingenious in his efforts to get a job. As the proceeds from the sale of our house in Scheveningen had been used up, my father knew he *had* to find a job and fast! So he went to the big yearly trade show in the center of Holland and looked for a company exhibiting the kind of butcher shop machinery he was familiar with. He found exactly what he was looking for and noticed lots of would-be customers waiting around for one of the (too few) salesmen. Without hesitation he moved behind the counter and started selling! By the end of the day he had sold *four* machines. The owners were so impressed that they hired him on the spot.

How I wish I could continue singing his praises! On second thought...*let me try:* He was an excellent bridge player and taught us the rudiments of the game at an early age. Every Saturday evening he and Mom played bridge with friends across the street, while Loek and I played bridge with Nora and Meta, their two daughters. As we were between eight and twelve years old it was not exactly serious bridge, but we had lots of fun.

My father was a fanatic when it came to bridge. He developed a phenomenal memory; he calculated where every card was and could remember what was played many hands ago. But... because of his hotheadedness that was not always a good thing: "How could you possibly play that *king*," he would yell at his partner, "that's the same stupid mistake you made a while back." He then proceeded to re-cap an entire hand played twenty minutes or so before.

He always told us that honesty was a virtue. But...he took being honest a little too far, to the point of being downright *rude*. He equated telling the truth with telling what was on his mind. "What a ridiculous hat you're wearing," he would say to a woman, or "Where in the world did you find that ugly rug?"

When my very embarrassed mother tried to hush him up his answer was always: "I'm only telling the truth."

My father was vehemently against my going to Portugal. "You're moving away from any happiness; you'll be an old maid when you come back," he cheerfully warned me. When Pop met John for the first time, in January of 1951, he was quite civil, almost friendly, until we told him we were going to get married.

He tried everything possible to make me change my mind. His first action was a call to the American Embassy in The Hague, to find out what an American should earn to support a family. I don't know to whom he spoke but the word came back: "If John doesn't make $1000 a month you'll be living in poverty!" Though John made a very good salary in Portugal, back in the States his pay was barely $400. He told Pop, that if what the embassy told him were true, 90% of the population in the U.S. would be living in poverty.

Over the years, no matter how often I told my father that John and I were very happy together, he kept on making snide remarks. "You married below your social status," he once wrote. I had to laugh out loud. "What social status?" I wrote him back, reminding him he was just a salesman working on commission. Ironically, John and I even loaned *him* money several years later to pay for accumulated income tax he had forgotten to put aside.

In 1955 my parents came to see us for six weeks in Beaufort, SC. This was their first visit to the States. I don't know in what kind of hovel my father had expected to find us, but he expressed surprise after seeing our house.

Though John didn't care much for fishing, he knew it was something my father loved. On the base you could check out a boat and fishing gear for free. So one Saturday the two of them set out for the ocean. After a short while Pop lit up one of his stinking cigars. When they got out in the open waters a storm started brewing. The motion of the boat combined with the thick cigar smoke made John sick. He tried bravely to hide how he felt. When he threw out his line the rod slipped out of his hand and disappeared into the water. My dad was fit as a fiddle and started to ridicule John: "You get sick in a little fishing boat? I thought you were a Marine!" Without saying a word John steered the boat back to the harbor. That was the last time he ever offered to go fishing with Pop. To make matters worse, he had to pay for the replacement of the lost equipment.

My parents' next visit was in 1959. "Your husband has bad manners," he told me during that time, "it's only the lower class that eats with a fork in their right hand."

I patiently tried to tell him that *all* Americans eat like that, even the president of the United States. According to my father, anything done differently from the Dutch way was considered bad manners. Nothing was ever *good* in the States, everything, according to him, was better in Holland.

In all fairness to him, I must mention another one of his *good* habits. Luke loved his grandfather, who knew literally every card game ever invented. Luke was an avid game player and ready to learn new ones. They sat for hours at the table playing cards. Once Luke said, "Do you know *go-fish?*" My father had never heard of it, so Luke proceeded to show him. "You call *dat* a game?" Pop groaned, "*Dat's* for people with no brain."

That reminds me of another card-playing story, which took place when Luke was about eleven. My father always played *meaty* games. You had to think. Gin rummy, for instance, was far below his standards.

One day he had taught Luke a new, quite complicated game. Pop, sitting with his back to the window, was winning constantly. Suddenly Luke realized he could very clearly see the reflection in the window of every card in his grandfather's hand. "Okay, Opa, I'm going to win the next game," Luke bragged. Knowing exactly what my father had in his hands, Luke proceeded to win game after game. Pop could not believe it. In his broken, heavily accented English he shouted out, "How is dat poe-ci-ble, dis cannot be poe-ci-ble!" When Luke confessed, Pop was not amused.

My father wrote me at least once a month, at times in a long-hand scribble, which took days to decipher, other times neatly typed. Invariably John became the focus of his letters. I don't think Pop ever forgave John for taking me away from Holland. Though he never openly admitted that, his remarks on the subject left no doubt.

"Do you realize," he once wrote, "that John snatched you away right from under my nose?" "What on earth do you mean by that?" I wrote back, "Would you have wanted me to stay with you and Mom my whole life?" "No," came the reply, "I was just trying to tell you that it still bothers me that John never asked me for your hand in marriage."

"Aha," John said after I translated my father's words, "so that's the crux of the matter." Till his death, Pop refused to accept that John and I were happy—*he never could be wrong.* My father's outbursts didn't bother John—he just ignored them. "He's an unhappy, bitter man—I feel sorry for him," he often told me. To John's credit he never said an unkind word to his father-in-law. On the contrary, he tried to cheer him up whenever he could.

Most of the time my mom visited us alone. However, after a heartbreaking tragedy in my Dutch family in 1965 (I'll tell you about in another chapter), John insisted they come together, at our expense, in 1966.

. During that stay John played a joke on my dad. My mother always brought *stroopwafels* for John from Holland, a delicious cookie John loved, a specialty of the town of *Gouda.* This time she had forgotten to order them in time, so she made arrangements with the baker to send a sealed tin directly to us. I can still hear John tell the story:

Paula and her mom had gone shopping, leaving me alone with my father-in-law, which was never an ideal situation. He rarely seemed to appreciate a conversation with me, so I surrounded him with magazines to pass the time away. Suddenly the doorbell rang. It was the UPS man dropping off a package.

I immediately recognized the shape: stroopwafels from Holland! It was about three in the afternoon and I quickly came up with an idea. I didn't tell Pop what had arrived but asked him if he would like a cup of tea. He accepted. While waiting for the water to boil I opened the tin, took one of the cookies out, put it on a plate and brought it to Pop, together with the tea, waiting for his reaction. Pop picked up his cup, saw the cookie and did a double take. He took the cookie in his hand, broke off a small piece and put it in his mouth. After repeating this procedure a few more times he turned to me and said in his broken English, "Dey are gute but not as gute as de Dutch!"

When John burst out laughing, my father asked what was so funny. After John told him the cookies were from Holland, Pop's only remark was that they *must have been stale.*

My father had a strong constitution. He was hardly ever sick, and never spent a day in a hospital. He smoked until late in life, drank more than he should, and always had a stash of chocolates by his side.

His mind was another matter; in his early eighties signs of dementia became evident, which accelerated in the following years.

He spent his last years in a nursing home, where he died in 1981 at the age of 92.

CHAPTER 33

My Wonderful Mom

My mother, Anthonia (aka To, Toos, or Toni), was an amazing woman. Though from simple upbringing she was very intelligent and had that indefinable quality: "class." It probably sounds awful to the un-initiated but she should never have married my father.

Although her parents had little money, her mother (my *Oma*) instilled the desire for knowledge in her children, to get a good education. My mom not only finished high school, but in the evening hours attended secretarial school. In spite of the fact that she was pretty, there was little time for socializing, no opportunity for dating.

When she was eighteen years old she started her first job as secretary for a large shipping concern. My father happened to be friends with one of the managers and occasionally dropped by to say hello. On one such visits the manager said, "Hey Polly, let me introduce you to my new secretary, Toos Pons.

Pop, an average looking thirty-two year old bachelor, started to talk to my mother and a day later sent her a bouquet of flowers. Next he asked her out, wined and dined her, and showered her with gifts. After six months of dating he asked her to marry him. My mom, nineteen years old, and totally inexperienced, accepted. Never having been in love she thought, well, this must be it. On July 21, 1920 they were married.

Over the years it became obvious they were complete opposites. Traits that stayed hidden during their courtship came to the foreground. While Mom had an abundant sense of humor, Pop was devoid of it. It greatly annoyed my immaculately groomed mother that her husband practiced rather poor hygiene. He was a difficult man to live with, had few close friends, and could be very demanding. It hurt Mom deeply that he treated Oma with disrespect. Pop's own mother detested her daughter-in-law, referring to her as *that child.* She made it clear she felt that her son *could have done much better.*

On May 9, 1921, their first son was born. As I've mentioned before, they had four children in all. Compensating for her disappointing marriage my mother doted on her children, becoming totally wrapped up in their lives. This had its unpleasant side effects—she was overly worried something bad might happen to us. We were the only children in school not allowed to go on fieldtrips as the *bus may be in an accident.* Once, when I was a teenager I asked if I could go sailing with friends. The answer was no, because *I might drown.* Sadly, all her planning and precautions for us did not spare her from disaster.

As I grew older, my appreciation for my mother turned into admiration. She was like a rock, holding the family together in hard times. When my father lost his business during the depression, Mom went to work and saw to it we never went without necessities. She was a terrific organizer and could do miracles with little money. She also had great taste in home-decorating. Shopping at antique markets and second-hand stores, she often found treasures overlooked by others, for just a few guilders.

In contrast to my father, who could never accept John, Mom was very happy about our marriage and learned to love him as her own son. John, from his side, adored his mother-in-law. Over the years he often encouraged her to visit with us.

Mom loved the ocean voyage on a luxury liner from Rotterdam to New York. She never got sea sick, even during big storms. Too bad New York City wasn't her final destination. As she was afraid of flying, four days and three nights in a Greyhound bus followed. In 1969, when trans-ocean voyages were discontinued, she had no other choice but to overcome her fear.

Her visits were not for just a few weeks; she often stayed for three or four months. My mother spoke good English, improving constantly by reading English books and magazines. John always spoiled her during those visits; he would surprise her with special treats, like bringing home her favorite dessert: lemon meringue pie. And he would say to me before she came, "When your mother is here, spend all the time you want with her; go shopping, take her to the City or whatever else she likes, I don't mind taking care of myself for a while."

I could never laugh with anyone as I did with my mom, to the point where at times we almost peed in our pants—somehow we had that effect on each other.

My mother loved everything about San Francisco, especially the big department stores. Though twenty-four years my senior, she could out-shop me. While I was ready to go home after four or five hours, she could have stayed all day. On one of our trips to the City we discovered "Scandia," a Swedish bakery on Powell Street. They had the yummiest pastries filled with almond paste. For lunch we went back for their delicious open-faced sandwiches. ("The Swedish," as we called it, became one of John's favorite places as well.)

Joyce and Luke loved their *Aba*. They felt deprived of grandparents. Around Thanksgiving and Christmas they often said, "All our friends go to their grandparents for dinner, the lucky bums." So the times they spend with Aba was always a celebration. John changed the name Aba into one of his pet names for her, which sounded like "Abazeenya," giving it a Portuguese flavor, meaning "dear little Aba." The name annoyed my dad: "Why does John call your mother Abyssinia?"

All four of us were sad each time Mom went back to Holland. John would comment, "Gee, I miss my ironed socks and underwear and all those great dinners." I hate to admit it but my mother was a much better cook and housekeeper than I ever was. During each visit she cleaned and re-organized every closet, cupboard, and cabinet in our house. Maybe that's why John was always eager to invite my mother to come and stay with us for months on end....

As she grew older, her trips to the States became more difficult. With all her medical needs she couldn't stay longer than four or five weeks. In Holland she was in constant pain. No medication helped. Amazingly, after just a few days with us her pain would disappear, reappearing after she returned home. The one positive aspect about her health was her mind—it stayed sharp and clear to the end.

My dear mother died in 1988 at the age of 87. John and I flew to Holland for her memorial service. I felt a deep loss. John had always been my best friend but my mom came in a close second.

I will be forever grateful to her for keeping all the letters I wrote her over the years. Without them I could never have written these stories.

Mom and Pop van Dalsum in 1954

Paula and her mom in Pleasant Hill—1959

CHAPTER 34

Bonifay Revisited

In 1961, six years after moving to California, we decided to take a trip to Florida during the summer for a week's visit with John's relatives. We chose a particular route in order to make short stopovers at the homes of friends and relatives on the way.

We drove one of those huge Chevy station wagons popular in that era. With the back seat down there was enough room for even an adult to stretch out. Seat belts didn't exist. The kids loved the wagon. They played games in the back, waved at passers-by and took naps in or atop a sleeping bag.

John's mother, age 77, had just remarried. She and her husband had purchased an old, barn-like house made entirely out of wood. It was devoid of paint and consequently looked quite shabby. John knew drastic and immediate actions were needed if he wanted to remedy this situation during our short stay. An idea started to form in his mind.

Through the grapevine he let it be known that there would be an *all day dinner* for friends and relatives, a feast with all the trimmings, at the new house the following Saturday.

The day before the party we went shopping. After spending over an hour at the "Piggly Wiggly," the local market, John stopped at the hardware store. Soon the wagon was loaded with gallons upon gallons of paint, brushes, long-handled rollers, buckets, ladders, you name it, anything he deemed necessary.

Southerners rarely pass up the chance for a free meal. Moreover, the Boswell clan wanted to say hello to their California relatives. They arrived in droves well before noon. Yes, we did let them have their fill first and they all seemed to have a good time. Then John spoke up: "Okay, you guys, now that you have all enjoyed the food, let's get to work. With this many people we can paint my mother's house in four or five hours." He started giving instructions. "Columbus, you and your sons start with the east side, T.B., Neils, Lester, and J.D. work together on the other side." After some initial reluctance, "Hey, you tricked us into this," everyone was cleaning, painting, and yes, chuckling about John's scheme. By the end of the day the entire house was painted.

Now that the house looked decent on the outside, John was determined to make life more comfortable for his mother on the inside. "I don't mind using the outhouse," she said after John's suggestion for indoor plumbing. John wouldn't listen; he insisted on an inside toilet for his aging mom and stepfather.

The man who called himself a "contractor" turned out to be not more than a (not so handy) handyman. In one of the rooms he enclosed an area to serve as bathroom. Walls were erected, a toilet was installed (with John doing most of the work), pipes were connected to the city sewer system, and soon the bathroom was ready for its first user. That's when we discovered that the carpenter had put the latch *on the outside of the bathroom*. "What the heck did you do *that* for?" John yelled at the man. The reply came: "I just figured someone can lock it on the outside and when the person is ready he can holler to be let out." After that logic John decided to give up and install the latch himself.

Most people in the Deep South, which included Bonifay, were still very racist in the early '60s, with strict segregation rules. This became obvious when we wanted to wash our clothes before our return trip. When we were about to enter a laundromat Joyce cried out, "Oh no, what are we going to do with all our *colored* clothes?" The sign on the door stated: "WHITES ONLY." Both our children were astonished when we explained the sad facts to them about the plight of Black people in the southern states. "Why don't they all move to California?" they asked innocently. If it had only been that simple....

There is one more Bonifay story worth mentioning. When travel by plane became cheaper, John often flew over for a week or ten-day visit with his relatives. In April of 1995 he invited two former POW buddies, a captain and a colonel, who lived within a four-hour drive, to get together with him in Bonifay. They called it the "Bonifay China Marine Reunion." It was front-page news in the "Holmes County Advertiser," a weekly newspaper John subscribed to. The headline read: **WWII VETERANS MEET IN BONIFAY.** A long story followed describing their plight during imprisonment.

That was not the last of it. Eight months later, at the end of December, an article appeared: **HIGHLIGHTS OF 1995.** One of the "highlights" mentioned was—you guessed it—the meeting of John and his buddies.

We concluded that not much was happening in Bonifay to call the meeting of the three men one of the highlights of the year.

CHAPTER 35

John the Teacher

At the end of March 1962, John became a credentialed teacher. He immediately accepted a job offer from the Mount Diablo School district to teach at El Monte Elementary School in Concord, starting with the beginning of the new school year. During the following two months he worked as a substitute teacher. As I had quit my real estate job, John's new income came as a great relief.

In September of that year John started his permanent job, teaching fourth grade. Typical of a principal assigning students to a brand-new teacher, he was given a class full of very difficult children. Previous teachers had given some up as "hopeless."

I went with John to the *Open House*, scheduled at the beginning of the school year. New teachers get introduced on that evening. Even after having taught just a few weeks, some parents told me they had never seen a teacher so popular with the students as "Mr. Boswell," that their children actually *liked* to come to school with him as teacher.

Other parents said they were impressed with the interesting (simple) science experiments he did with the class. They also told him how much the kids enjoyed it when he brought his guitar to school and sang songs with them.

Though bringing gifts for teachers was discouraged, John came home with lots of "loot" on the last day of the school year, in June of 1963. The best gift was a letter from a mother that said, "Mr. Boswell, I have thanked God in my prayers many times that you were my son's teacher. I wish you strength for the future, so that you can continue your good work." John was very touched by that letter. The boy had been an impossible child and few teachers had paid much attention to him. Under John's guidance he started to do well and began to enjoy learning. More recognition came the following year, when "his" students, now in fifth grade, kept up their good grades and interest in learning.

To make some much needed extra money, John accepted a home-teaching assignment in the fall of '66—one hour each day after school for the rest of the semester. Not an easy job, as the student, nine-year old Bob, lived quite a distance away. Instead of coming home before 4:00 p.m. John now didn't get back until close to six o'clock. We were both happy when that assignment was over. We had missed our afternoon cups of tea together.

A few weeks later John received a copy of a letter sent by Bob's parents to the Mount Diablo School District. They thanked the District sincerely for the home teaching and went on to say:

> Mr. John Boswell, 4th grade teacher at the El Monte School, was sent to our home each day. He is the finest teacher we have had the pleasure to observe. Mr. Boswell is enthusiastic, sincere, and has a love and concern for children that is outstanding. He immediately perceived Bob's problems and took a personal interest in helping him overcome them. He has inspired Bob to think for himself and has instilled in him a desire to succeed. We are certain Mr. Boswell spends endless hours preparing extra learning opportunities to make each subject more interesting for his students.

After five years of classroom teaching John became a *resource teacher*. In that capacity, instead of having his own class, he worked with different students each day, both under and over-achievers. He continued in that function until he retired in the winter of 1978, for a total of fifteen years of teaching.

Many times during the rest of his life John received notes from former students. He even corresponded with some after they were married and had children of their own.

After John's death, in September of 2003, more than forty years after he started teaching, my family and I received very touching condolences from grateful former students. Here are some excerpts. From "Nina":

> *I have not seen Mr. Boswell since 1967, yet he had a memorable impact on my life. His obituary shares much information regarding his life experiences that influenced who he became, yet only two brief sentences speak to the fact that he was a teacher, and influenced many students, making them better people for having spent time in his classrooms.*
>
> *I don't remember a lot of details from that year, but I do remember that Mr. Boswell always treated his students with respect and helped to build our self-confidence. He set high standards and challenged us to do our best work. He taught us to ask questions about our world and made learning fun and interesting. I have admired him all these years knowing that he helped to lay the groundwork for many years of learning to follow. The world has lost a great person and I am fortunate to have shared just one year of Mr. Boswell's 83 years on this earth.*

And from another student, "Wendy":

> *Mr. Boswell was my 4th grade teacher at El Monte Elementary. I think the year was 1964. Mr. Boswell made a deep impression in my mind and in my heart. It amazes me that he was such a kind loving man after reading about his time in the military. I adored Mr. Boswell, in fact my mother to this day remembers my 4th grade year because it was always "Mr. Boswell this" and "Mr. Boswell that." He was loved by many many kids that had him for a teacher and he will always, always be in my heart.*

I also treasured the condolence letter from one of John's fellow-teachers:

> *John was a very special man. I can well remember many wonderful assemblies with John and his guitar leading the singing. My first grade class was especially thrilled to have him as their teacher all day when I was on jury duty for four days.*
>
> *We had so many laughs during lunch hour. John had many stories to tell about peanut-farming and growing up in the South.*

The many tributes we received about John after his death warmed my heart. To have touched so many lives and influenced so many young people is something very unique and will live on in generations to come.

CHAPTER 36

My Sister Toto

Toto (short for Anthonia, named after my mother), was seven years my junior. Because of that age difference we were never very close while I was a teenager. However, during my two-year stay in Portugal, we exchanged long letters. A few years later, when I spent almost a year in Holland with Joyce, we became great friends.

Toto was often sick. When she was only seven years old she spent three months in a children's hospital. At the age of twelve she was near death from what was first diagnosed as meningitis. She survived it all, never losing her zest for life.

I was somewhat shy as a child. Toto, on the other hand, was very outgoing, exuberant even, with an abundant love for people and animals alike. I still feel bad when I think about her pet bunny she had in Scheveningen when she was just a little girl. One week we were so short of money and consequently, food, that we had the rabbit for dinner. Toto was terribly upset and didn't eat for days.

Though she never cared much for school she excelled in all physical activities. She played hockey and tennis with great intensity and enthusiasm.

When she was about eighteen, Toto developed serious intestinal problems. My parents took her to many different doctors and specialists. She underwent numerous tests, was on a multitude of medications, and a special, bland diet. At times she had to stay in bed for weeks. Toto hated to be sick. The moment she felt better, though told to take it easy, she went right back to her favorite sports activities.

She and my mom were extremely close and remained so after she married and moved to a small town about sixty miles from The Hague. Within eight years she and her husband, Hans Tuyt, had three children.

Toto's health didn't improve over the years. Instead, it deteriorated further. She was eventually diagnosed as suffering from a severe case of ulcerative colitis. In November of 1964 she was hospitalized for an indefinite period. Her doctor ordered a series of tests, bed rest and a very strict diet. Many agonizing weeks followed with little or no improvement. We all prayed daily for her recovery and tried to stay positive. As the cost of overseas phone calls at that time was exorbitant my mother wrote me two or three times a week to keep me posted on the latest developments. When she did call me on January 2, I knew the news could not be good. I was told Toto had undergone surgery and was in a coma.

Not ready to give up, her body kept on fighting. Against the doctor's predictions she woke up from the coma and seemed to be improving. Our hopes soared. Was she going to make it? Then...a relapse. Daily we lived between hope and despair. I was afraid to pick up the phone for fear of what I was going to hear. A week later more surgery was performed. Though she survived that as well, she was now in critical condition.

On January 18 the phone rang. When I heard it was an operator from Western Union with a telegram, all I could think was, oh no, don't let it be *that*. The operator was very compassionate. With concern in her voice she said, "I'm afraid I have bad news." Then she relayed the words I had hoped I would never have to hear: "Toto has died."

After surviving the second operation she had died from a blood clot. Twenty-two years after my brother Loek met his horrible death, my parents lost their youngest child at the age of thirty-three. Toto's children were two, four, and six years old.

I remembered my mother saying after Loek's death: "One thing I know with certainty; this is the worst thing I will have to endure in all my life." It's good she didn't know then what lay ahead.

When I received the telegram with the devastating news my first thought was, how is Mom going to survive this, how can my parents keep on living?

I called my mother to tell her I would be there for the funeral. "No, please don't come," she pleaded, "It would worry me sick thinking that your plane may crash."

In one of her next letters she wrote about the words my brother Hans had spoken during the memorial service. He had mentioned what a totally selfless person Toto had been, spreading love all around her, always ready for anyone needing her help, thinking up little surprises for friends to cheer them up, *offering* assistance before being asked, never worrying about inconveniencing herself.

Those words made me re-evaluate my own life, realizing my shortcomings. Yes, it's easy to do anything in your power for your loved ones, but I had failed dismally thus far in reaching out to outsiders, even friends. To put it bluntly: *I had not been much of a Christian.* I truly felt I wanted to change.

Little things that used to upset me suddenly seemed unimportant. When Joyce broke one of my favorite plates without a comment from me, Luke said, "Gee Mom, aren't you going to yell at her?" A month before I had worried about a few gray hairs. Now it all seemed so trivial.

I cried a lot those first few weeks, not just for my own loss but even more so for my parents, especially my mother. John and the children showed their support in many ways, sometimes by taking work out of my hands like cooking breakfast or dinner, and other times by writing little notes to me expressing their feelings: "We're happy when you're happy and we're sad when you're sad because we love you."

It struck me how some of my friends understood my feelings so well, while others had no clue. While carpooling for a while with a friend I had told her about the devastating events of the last few months. Several weeks after Toto's death she was driving while I sat next to her, lost in thought about my mother, wondering how she was dealing with her loss. My friend suddenly turned to me and said, "What are you looking so sad for *now*?" In other words, hey, you've had your two weeks of grief—snap out of it!

My mother, "Mimi" to the Dutch grandchildren, stayed on at Toto's house caring for her son-in-law and the children until a permanent nanny could be found. It actually was good therapy for her, as she was too busy to think about her grief and she didn't want the little children to see her cry. Over the years an incredible closeness developed between her and Toto's kids. She became like a second mother to them, even in adulthood.

Right after Toto's death I knew I had to find something, anything, to help my mom. I sent her some booklets on grief my pastor had given me, and kept looking for other available literature that could help both my parents. That's when I discovered the books Catherine Marshall had written after her husband, well known pastor Peter Marshall, had died at a young age. The first book I sent was "To Live Again." Next came "Beyond Ourselves." In our letters my mother and I discussed these books at length. Through them she slowly began to learn how to find peace within herself and how to pray for strength.

She visited with us many more times over the years. It made me happy to see she could laugh again and enjoy life once more but I knew that Loek and Toto would always be in her thoughts and in her heart.

Toto van Dalsum — Tuyt
August 17, 1931 — January 18, 1965

CHAPTER 37

A Late Bloomer

Not long after John received his college degree at age 42, he started to urge me on to do the same. "Give it a try, I'm sure you're going to love it, and I'll help you with the kids and the house." As John's enthusiasm and sincere desire for my higher education was somewhat infectious, I decided to look into the matter.

Five years earlier, as you already know, I had taken just one class, in real estate, which had brought great results, but going *full time* or even just part time, was a whole different ballgame. Thinking back of my high school years—7th through 11th grade—I had hated most anything about school, homework in particular. So should I now, at age 37, take the plunge? Would I suddenly *like* to study? And *what subjects?* While living under German occupation I had developed a strong dislike of the German language, so I scratched that possibility.

I perused the offerings for the coming semester at the local community college. Once you know a few languages, I figured, it's never hard to learn new ones, so I decided to take a class in—of all things—*Russian.* Another class that seemed interesting was *Public Speaking* ("Speech"), and for no reason whatsoever I also enrolled in *Economics.* Not a full load but plenty to start.

The Russian class turned out to be far more difficult than I expected; I knew Germanic and Romance languages but this

Slavic tongue was a different matter. Practically no words could be traced to any of the languages I spoke. To learn vocabulary I hung lists in all my kitchen cabinets. Each time I opened a cabinet door the words were staring me in the face.

Getting a passing grade was not the only result that class brought. The teacher, a multi-linguist, suggested I attend his German and French level III classes. If I did well he promised to let me take a test to get full credit for levels I and II in both. A lot of units just thrown into my lap! Though hesitant at first about German, I followed his advice. I dropped Economics and by the end of the semester was well underway to completing my lower division requirements.

To John's great delight I absolutely loved my studies. Besides, not wanting to look stupid in classes with students half my age, I studied so hard I got mostly A's. My self-confidence soared. I decided to become a high school foreign language teacher.

In the speech class I discovered that I was actually sort of a ham; I loved to speak before audiences. My teacher encouraged me to participate in the semi-annual college-wide speech contest. To my utter disbelief I won first place.

At the end of the second semester I added another trophy: the "Norseman Award" in Foreign Languages. I often wondered why I had been so anti-school and anti-studying as a teenager. Why had I wasted five years of my life?

John was overjoyed that he had made the suggestion for me to take classes. I'm quite certain our friends and neighbors got tired of hearing John brag about his wife's accomplishments.

Though he rarely made a comment, I'm sure he was less thrilled with my cooking endeavors during my college years. As studying took up a lot of my spare time, making dinner became somewhat of an afterthought. Joyce knew my "scheme" at dinnertime. I would always keep some delicious store-bought dessert in the freezer, for those times dinner was so lousy that a good dessert might offer some consolation. One time when I put a wonderful dessert on the table Joyce whispered in my ear, "Gee Mom, dinner wasn't *that* bad."

Once I baked a cake for a *cake walk* at the kids' school. John looked at it longingly and said to Joyce, "Hmm, that looks and smells delicious." "So you like pineapple upside-down cake, Dad?" "Well," John quipped, "I don't really remember, I haven't tasted one in years." That remark made me feel so guilty I quickly made a ready-mix package-cake for Joyce's school and kept the upside-down cake for us.

After my fairly easy two junior college years, I now had to prepare myself for a new challenge: UC Berkeley. I got a challenge all right, but not the way I anticipated. My first few months at Cal Berkeley coincided with the arrival of Mario Savio and his Free Speech Movement (FSM). Huge crowds gathered on the steps of the administration building, protesting the refusal of University leaders to let students engage in any kind of politics on the campus. For many weeks there were demonstrations everywhere, sit-ins, and attempts to take over entire buildings, resulting in three hundred arrests. To get to my classes I had to cross picket lines. One of my German teachers, an elderly woman who had lived under the Nazi Regime was too scared to set foot on the campus. Everything was in turmoil.

An offshoot of the FSM started to display the "four letter word" on big banners. I was so naïve, I had never heard the F-word before and had to ask John what it meant!

Near the end of the semester, to everyone's great relief, the movement died

The rest of my years at Cal were a lot less eventful. I did enjoy every minute of my studies; I had come to love not only the German language (my major) itself but even more so its literature, with all its influential movements. After studying Thomas Mann's books at length, it was a real thrill to take a seminar led by *his son*, Michael Mann. (He committed suicide several years later.) I became so exhilarated by all this new learning, this—pardon the cliché—broadening of my horizons, I could have become a spokesperson at high schools proclaiming the importance of a college education.

I met many interesting people. One of them was a young blind girl with a seeing-eye dog. Walking along Telegraph Avenue on the way to the campus with her one day I expressed my amazement at how the dog knew exactly where to go and where to stop. I told her how lucky she was to have the animal as her guide. "Not always," came her surprising reply, "Sometimes when the weather is really wonderful I feel like skipping class, but my dog, knowing exactly where I am supposed to go, *won't let me stay outside.* She'll pull and pull on the leash until I finally give up and go."

Close to the end of my studies I set one more goal for myself: I wanted to be invited into the Phi Beta Kappa Society. I became a little "sneaky," if you can call it that, to accomplish this feat. Just a year earlier, for a better chance at being hired as teacher, I had added classes in Spanish, a new language for me. Having a lot in common with Portuguese and French I had no problem with the grammar. However, to add Spanish as an official *minor*, I had to take several literature classes, conducted entirely in Spanish. A daunting task! So I waited till the very last term. Weeks before those Spanish courses ended, I got my "Key." Better yet, I got my degree in German with a minor in French and Spanish.

I taught for ten years, teaching German and an occasional Spanish or French class at a local high school. Some of these years were not devoid of drama.

As all teachers had to share in chaperoning sports events, I signed on, during my first year, as substitute chaperone to the school's ski club. In contrast to John, who wasn't the slightest bit interested in learning how to ski, I had always wanted to try it. Here's my chance! I thought. "You're crazy," my husband warned. "You'll come home with a broken leg." This was in

February. We already had a flight booked for the whole family to go to Europe for eleven weeks during summer vacation.

I rented the necessary equipment and set out in a school bus, with about thirty students and one other chaperone, on a four-hour trip to a ski resort. After taking one lesson in the morning I looked longingly at the skiers zooming down the hill. It seemed so easy! So after lunch I bought a lift ticket and soon found myself at the top, ready to schuss down. Though a little hesitant at first, after a few minutes I was getting the hang of it until...I was going too fast! How was I going to stop? The beginner's lesson hadn't covered that. Frantically looking around, I noticed a snowy meadow off to the side. That snow would automatically slow me down, I reasoned. Yes, it did, but so abruptly that I fell. The cheap rental skis didn't release. I fell over while my legs were still attached to the skis, which were firmly embedded in the snow, if you can get the picture. A searing pain set in. People stopped and called the ski patrol. They tied me like a papoose to a basket. My earlier wish to zoom down the hills was now fulfilled but not the way I had envisioned. I was scared to death.

"Better wait with X-rays until you're home," they told me at the first-aid station. The four hours back in that school bus were a nightmare. On my arrival John was called at once. To my great relief he didn't say, "I told you so." Instead he rushed me to the hospital where I soon heard I had broken both the tibia and fibula in my left leg. How could I have been that stupid? I kept thinking and worse: Can I still make the trip to Europe? Yes, I did make the trip but I hobbled all over Europe with my leg in a knee-high cast.

The rest of my teaching years weren't that eventful. I had some good times as well as disappointments. To those students *willing* to learn I was—I think—a good teacher but compared to John, the humanitarian, who lived and breathed for his pupils, I felt somewhat of a failure. I'm sure that after my demise my family isn't going to receive touching letters from students I taught thirty and forty years ago.

My teaching however, became another link in the chain of my life. Together with some enthusiastic German students I organized an Oktoberfest at the school. In Dirndls and Lederhosen the students performed "Schuh-plattler" dances; we had our own student "oompah" band, all sorts of German food, and finally, lots of game booths. For those booths we needed *prizes*. These inexpensive trinkets proved to be very hard to find. I knew that many churches and elementary schools in the area organized carnivals for fundraising, requiring prizes. An idea started to form in my mind.

Paula the German teacher

CHAPTER 38

Thrift

When you grow up with "thrift" it sticks with you, no matter how much money you eventually amass. In our earlier years of marriage we *had* to be frugal and find clever ways to add to our income. It became sort of a *sport.*

The two of us had different ways to accomplish this. John hardly ever spent money on himself. The twenty-dollar bill he put in his wallet at the beginning of the month for unforeseen expenses was always still there 30 days later. When he worked at the *Beach* on Parris Island he often came home with heaps of oysters he had gathered. They provided quite a few free meals for John, while the children and I were just as happy with a meatball dinner. When there was surplus paint on the base or equipment with minor defects ready for tossing, he gratefully took that home for future use. But I had learned not to ask him to pay with a "half off" coupon; that embarrassed him.

My mother and I were just the opposite—we didn't mind flaunting our thrifty ways. Each time Mom visited with us she became my cohort. While I was a student at Cal Berkeley, the "food" section appeared in the *San Francisco Chronicle* on Wednesdays, literally filled with "cents-off" coupons. As we had discovered, some stores would cash them in even without us buying the product. They simply deducted the value of all coupons combined from our purchases. So every Wednesday my mother came with me to the campus. While I attended classes she would go to the cafeteria, the student union, or wherever students were gathering. Lots of students bought newspapers. Keeping only the parts they were interested in, they quickly discarded the entire food section. My mom was lurking around. The moment she saw such an abandoned paper she grabbed it. When we met again after classes she usually had gathered between two and three dozen papers. One Thanksgiving we had enough coupons to get our entire turkey dinner for free.

Then there was the radio "auction," a promotion from some local businesses. You could bid for products with *register receipts* from the participating merchants. I was made aware of this when we bought a new refrigerator. "Remember to save the receipt," we were told, followed by an explanation of the procedure.

The next morning I turned on the radio at 9:00 a.m. The program lasted thirty minutes. "As our first item this morning we have a set of deluxe ballpoint pens, for a total of $20 in receipts," came the announcement. The first person calling in became the "winner"; no bidding or anything of the sort.

I soon realized I had to be faster. Before even knowing what the next item was, I started dialing all but one number. "Now we have a very special offering: two complete steak dinners with drinks and dessert for a total of $50." Before the announcer was completely finished I dialed the last number and *bingo,* the steak dinners were mine, followed by a large bottle of "My Sin" perfume, a transistor radio and a certificate for a dozen Simplicity patterns.

My receipts were now depleted. It was such a heady feeling to get all that stuff for free, that I started to think of new ways to find more receipts without having to buy anything. As luck would have it, a supermarket was added to the list of sponsors. Luke still remembered forty years later how he and Joyce would scrounge for receipts discarded by shoppers, usually close to the cash registers or in the parking lot. For weeks I kept on "winning" all sorts of loot, including four tickets to "Babes in Toyland," a children's musical in the "Theatre in the Round" in San Carlos. The only wished-for prize that eluded me, for lack of enough receipts, was a weekend stay at the Highlands Inn in Carmel.

Roos Atkins, a nice men's store, once had the misfortune to advertise something like: "Try our new crew socks! Guaranteed for life never to wear out." Men's socks are usually marked to fit sizes 9 to 11. Luke with his size 12 wore out socks in a matter of months. I bought three pair. When several months later they were full of holes, I traded them in for new ones. Over the next five years I kept on exchanging old for new. The store kept its promise; they never hesitated to make the trade. Whenever Joyce was with me, it embarrassed her to the point she would say to me, "You go ahead, I'll hide out somewhere." John joked later that I contributed to the demise of the store.

Frankly, I could write hundreds of pages on how we saved money. John, at times, thought I took being thrifty too far by becoming a "krent," Dutch slang for *miser,* or to put it more bluntly: *cheapskate.* Once we received a package on December 22 from distant relatives, containing a few small gifts. We had never talked about a gift exchange so my immediate thought was, why send them anything in return, it wouldn't get there in time anyway. John looked at me expectantly. "What's the matter," I asked. "I know exactly what you're thinking. You're trying to find a reason not to have to send them anything back." How well he knew me! Reluctantly, I went shopping for return gifts.

Having no money for expensive clothes didn't prevent me from *looking.* On one such a trip, not long after arriving in the Bay Area, I spotted a suit—brown tweed with a mink collar—that I absolutely *had* to have. The only way to buy it, in that pre-credit card era, was to put it on *lay-away.* This meant I couldn't take it home until I paid the exorbitant price of $69. My brain started to work frantically; where was I going to get that much money? Suddenly I remembered: I still had about $300 in gift items left over from "Paula's Gift Shop" inventory. To whom could I sell it?

I went to various retail shops, offering my wares. A few were willing to take some on consignment. After several more trips one store owner actually *bought* twenty dollars worth—a beginning! Then he mentioned, "I often have customers looking for cute aprons." He promised to buy a dozen if he liked what I made.

In Beaufort I had been quite successful selling aprons with attached fingertip towels. I bought some bright-colored remnants and towels on sale, took out the sewing machine, and went to work. A few days later I received $18. Within a week I received calls that several of the consigned gift items had sold. Less than three weeks later I paid for the suit.

How is John going to react, I wondered. He was not used to my making such extravagant purchases. As soon as he got home I modeled the suit for him. "Where did you get that?" he marveled, "It looks great on you, I love it!" I felt relief until he said, "How much did it cost?" "Well," I hesitated, "you might not want to know." He laughed. "Then don't tell me; I really don't care how much it was, it looks terrific and you deserve something beautiful." I was so happy with his reaction that I promised I'd cook him one of his favorite southern meals: black-eyed peas with cornbread, and banana pudding for dessert.

CHAPTER 39

A Hundred Dollar Windfall

In 1966, as part of my studies for a teaching credential, I took a few summer classes at UC Berkeley. Though still a year before what was to be dubbed the "summer of love," hippies were rampant on the campus, often barefoot, and dressed in the most bizarre clothes.

One of my classes, led by Professor Stone, came right after lunch. Instead of starting with the lecture Dr. Stone said one afternoon, "Let me tell you what happened to me during the lunch break." After he proceeded to relate his story, we all laughed—it was funny.

I had been wracking my brain how to make some extra money, when several weeks later an idea popped into my mind: *I should send Dr. Stone's story to Reader's Digest!* John, the composition specialist, helped me write the story in the best way possible: short and to the point. I sent it in and promptly forgot about it. Eight months later I received the following letter:

Dear Mrs. Boswell,

We're pleased to enclose our check for $100 in payment to you for the attached item, scheduled for page 93 of the April Digest.

Saying that we were elated is an understatement. John immediately remarked, "Now honey, I want this to be *your* money. Don't even dream of using it to buy groceries or something practical for the house." I bought a light yellow, much-needed, raincoat, which I had admired from afar but didn't think I could afford.

Not to keep you in suspense any longer, here's the story, verbatim:

> *After a swim in the pool at the University of California's Berkeley campus, a professor found that his socks and shoes were missing from the locker room. Since the weather was mild, he decided to walk barefoot to a nearby shoe store, attired in a business suit, white shirt, and tie. He was somewhat disappointed when no one gave him a second glance. The climax came, though, when the clerk, after fitting him with shoes and socks, inquired coolly, "Would you like to wear them, sir, or shall I wrap them up?*

> *Contributed by Mrs. John R. Boswell*

That's not the end of the story. What I didn't know before, Dr. Stone and I had a mutual acquaintance: Howard Carter, a school principal in Martinez. On our next visit with the Carters I told them, "Guess what, I got a hundred bucks for a story from Reader's Digest!" They didn't read the magazine so I told them the details. They immediately burst out laughing. "That was *you*? That's incredible!" Just a few weeks before, they had had dinner with Dr. Stone and his wife. The professor had been quite indignant, telling them about his experience on the campus and how, *the same day it happened*, he had sent his version of the story to the R.D. and never got an answer. "And here I open the April Reader's Digest and read *my* story, sent in by some woman I've never heard of."

John and I thought it was hilarious. And we needed the money a lot more than Dr. Stone.

CHAPTER 40

"Danville — One Acre Lot for Sale"

That classified ad, listing a price far below the going rate, practically leaped out at me. Ever since we were married we had dreamed about owning a home out in the country on an acre or so of land. The ad appeared early in 1966. Just a few months before, we had sold our last investment rental, which resulted in our bank balance climbing to $6000.

I immediately called the listing broker to see if it was still available. My next question (as I still had a valid broker's license) was: would he "cooperate," as it's known in the trade, meaning, would I get part of the commission, selling it to myself. Both replies were affirmative.

I'm surprised I didn't get a speeding ticket. I literally *flew* from Concord to Danville. As I was acting as broker, the listing salesman didn't offer to show me where the land was. After he made a rough map I was on my own.

Following several failed efforts I finally found Kuss Road, a steep, narrow, winding road. Many pieces of vacant land, a few houses here and there. Where was *my* land? I looked at the map again and saw the house number of the people across the street. Then I noticed a small *for sale* sign. I got out of the car and proceeded up a hill. I became a little skeptical. *How could you build on such an incline?* After climbing for several minutes, to my great relief, the ground became quite level. Trying to catch my breath upon so much exertion, I turned around to sit down on the dirt and literally *gasped.* Mount Diablo, in all its glory, lay before my eyes. It was an incredible, unobstructed panoramic view. I immediately knew: *I have to have this land.* I jumped up, ran, almost rolled, down the hill and raced to the broker's office.

There was a hitch, however. The land was offered at a reduced price, as the owner needed money *that same week.* Moreover, we had to buy the property "as is." There was a chance we wouldn't be able to build on it for a few years, until sewers were approved for the area. I didn't care—we didn't yet have the money to build anyway. I put down a deposit and signed an offer to buy: $6000 down—our entire savings—and the remainder on a note.

I called John at his school during lunch hour. "You never guess what I bought this morning," I screamed excitedly and proceeded to tell him what I had done. John, as always, completely trusted my judgment and was as thrilled as I was. "That's fabulous, honey," was his reply, "you know, you're really something else!"

We weren't quite there yet. The buyer wanted *two thousand dollars more in cash.* We borrowed on our life insurance, the quickest way to get money in a hurry. I was so worried something would go wrong that I personally did all the running around to get the deal closed. Within a week we were the very happy and excited owners of 1.10 acre of choice Danville land. And…I received a commission check for $400. It was the best investment we ever made.

Almost every weekend we went to see our land. We would sit, staring at the view, and dream. Next we would drive through Danville, in awe that some day soon we would live in this wonderful, quaint town.

At times Luke and his friends came along. They explored the land, hunting for fossils of seashells and whalebones in the crumbling sandstone rocks. We were surprised to learn that many millions of years ago the entire area had been under water as part of the Pacific Ocean.

Three years later the sewers were approved and we got permission to build. *Our life-long dream was getting closer....*

CHAPTER 41

A Family of Squatters

After several years of planning, consulting architects, mortgage brokers, and contractors, the building of our new home had finally begun.

We sold our house in Concord quicker than expected, which brought new problems—the buyers had stipulated a move-in date of June 15, 1969. Our home in Danville was far from ready; a lot of rain and occasional strikes had made it impossible to meet the completion date. It would have been expensive and inconvenient to rent for a few months and move twice, so: *ready or not, here we come!* Thank heaven for California's rainless summers.

With the help of friends we moved our belongings, going back and forth numerous times in a *pick-up truck.* Most of our large furniture was put in the (unfinished) garage.

Here's what the house looked like on moving in: there was no front door; though the redwood siding was in place, inside there were no walls yet, just the two-by-four framework. As the builder needed water and electricity, he hooked up lines for us as well, for a toilet and a refrigerator. We hung old drapes around the open bathroom area and whenever you *had to go* you would yell, "throne," announcing you didn't want anyone near. I'm not at all sure it was *legal* to live in such an unfinished house; we just didn't ask anyone.

All four of us lived and slept in the two downstairs bedrooms-to-be. Our furniture consisted of a TV (we saw Neil Armstrong's first moon landing amid all this chaos), a couch, a few chairs, and beds for John and me. The children slept on chaise lounges. We had no showers or cooking facilities. My super clean husband rigged up a kind of showerhead at the end of a garden hose and took ice-cold showers every morning. The children and I weren't that brave; we took occasional showers at friends' houses.

We ate breakfast at the IHOP in Walnut Creek, one of the few restaurants serving breakfast in the late sixties. I became familiar with every crepe on their menu. At home we ate sandwiches, lots and lots of them. Once in a while we went out for dinner.

Then the word came: "The sheetrock contractors are coming." *We had to get out.* For the next two weeks we slept in sleeping bags on the second floor deck. I wrote my mother: *I must say it's sort of thrilling to wake up at night and see the stars above you.*

Soon the walls and ceilings were ready for painting. To save a mere $800, we had decided to do all indoor painting ourselves. What we hadn't realized and were shocked to learn: *this included sanding down, staining, and finishing the kitchen and bathroom cabinets, and all the doors.* We had never done that kind of work before. What a miserable, rotten job! And the results were nothing to write home about—a very hard earned $800 indeed. The children both helped painting walls and Luke became an expert lining all closet floors with cedar strips.

Little by little we got more conveniences. Our first hot shower! All the kitchen appliances! And we immensely enjoyed sitting on the side deck, watching the pool take shape. Yes, the pool! With both of us teaching (my first year), we had been able to save up enough to afford that luxury.

At last, three months after moving in, the house was finished. Luke took his first dive in the pool. Normalcy had returned.

We were totally broke, but other than the mortgage we had no debt. And our life-long dream had finally become a reality.

CHAPTER 42

Mabel Kuss

When we first moved to Kuss Road I was not too thrilled with the name. Most people pronounce it "Cuss." It's actually a German word—meaning *kiss*—and doesn't have an equivalent sound in English. However, it's perfectly acceptable to say "Koos" with the "oo" sound of <u>loot</u>. Over the years, a few homeowners suggested a name change but the history associated with the name won out.

Anyway, I didn't think it was a great name until I met (almost) ninety years old *Mabel Kuss,* living in the quaint house at the foot of the road. Her pioneer father had owned hundreds of acres, stretching on one end all the way to Danville Blvd. Mabel's two sisters inherited parcels down the road. They named the streets after their husbands: Harper Lane and Cordell Drive.

Mabel loved company. She latched on to us the moment we moved to Danville. She had a million stories—about growing up in the Valley where one year she was chosen *prune queen,* and about the feud between her and her sister who had *snatched her beau away from her.* Never married, she called herself a "maiden lady." There were detailed stories about her cat. She had named it *Bambie* as, according to her, it looked just like a fawn. She cherished that cat as if it were a child.

Mabel already lived on Kuss Road when Eugene O'Neill, the famous playwright, built on top of the hill in the late thirties. O'Neill's daughter, Oona, was married to Charlie Chaplin. "Charlie often came to visit," Mabel told us, "and would go downtown to Elliott's Bar. He sometimes drank so much they had to push him up the hill in a wheelbarrow."

Mabel, with her knowledge about the entire valley, was a valuable asset and active member of the local historical society. She was less interested in mundane tasks like house cleaning. Her house was full of clutter. Stacks and stacks of paper were piled up on every table; some were tax returns from ten years back.

Good-hearted John, feeling sorry for her, uttered these fateful words: "Mabel, if you ever need any help, give me a call." He had no idea what he was getting into.

Her first call was about going to the market. "Just write me out a list, Mabel, and I'll get it for you." Oh no, Mabel wanted John to take her, so she could make her own selections. At the market John got a cart. "Let me have that, John." No matter how hard John pleaded she insisted on pushing the cart. John, in his early fifties, strong and healthy looking, sheepishly walked alongside the cart, feeling the disapproving stares of other shoppers. (As we got older, we realized Mabel needed the *support* the cart gave her but was too proud to admit that.)

One day, while John was right in the middle of a big project in the yard, I got a call from Mabel asking if John could "help her" pull weeds. John didn't want to stop in the middle of his work, so he turned to fifteen-year-old Luke: "Why don't *you* go and help the old lady?" That's the last thing Luke wanted to do on a beautiful Saturday morning. However, knowing his dad, he knew arguing would be useless. So off he went, hoe in hand. He had some choice words when he returned: "That woman is nuts! She threw my hoe aside and told me to pull her weeds by hand, *one by one*. And when I started to yank them out she told me I did it all wrong. She stood next to me the whole time, watching. I don't want to go there ever again!"

Next thing we knew we had a crying Mabel on the phone. "John, it's Mabel. I'm so upset, Bambie died last night and I don't know what to do. Can you come and help me?"

They sat down together to discuss the action to be taken. Mabel, grieving over her kitty, had no answers. One thing for sure, she didn't want the cat to just be stuck in the ground. John was looking at his watch, thinking he'd better come up with an idea or he'd be there till midnight. He finally said, "Why don't I build a little coffin for Bambie?" Mabel perked up. "Oh, that's wonderful, John; I knew you would have an answer!"

John scrounged around for some wood in our garage and built a box big enough to hold Bambie. Mabel was happy. The saga of course, continued. "Let's go into the yard to find the best place for the grave." John obediently dug the hole at the indicated spot. Together they proceeded to bury the animal. "I don't know how to thank you enough," she said before John went home.

Several days later the phone rang. It was Mabel. "John, you remember where we buried Bambie? When the meter reader came by he walked *right over her grave*. Maybe there's too much traffic in that part of the garden. Would you mind terribly to put her somewhere more secluded?"

John's brother Jake (aka J.D.), had just arrived from Florida. "Jake, let's go and dig up a dead body." "What?!" Jake screamed. John explained and the two went over to Mabel's. They dug up the box and put it exactly where Mabel was pointing.

A week went by. *Ring, ring,* Mabel again. "You know John, sometimes I have a hard time knowing exactly where the grave is. Could you build a little picket fence around it?" John obliged; what else could he do—tell her she was a pain in the neck? Again, he received profuse thanks for his efforts.

Several weeks went by. John heaved a sigh of relief... *Not so fast, John, it ain't over yet!* Yes, she called him again. "I hate to say this but Bambie's grave looks so barren. Do you think you could put some flowers inside the picket fence?"

That was the end of the cat story. She did ask him many more times to help her with small chores. Each time John left for her house he would say to me, "If I'm not home within an hour, call Mabel and tell her that you need me."

There's one more tale about Mabel worth recalling. When Mabel turned *ninety* John felt we should take her out to lunch for her birthday. One of our favorite restaurants was the "Elegant Bib" in Alamo. In addition to the excellent food, they advertised with a *free lunch, including dessert and drinks on your ninetieth birthday.*

How could we miss? We picked Mabel up and set out for Alamo. "Mabel, you can order anything your heart desires, food and drink, everything," John told her. She didn't have to hear that invitation twice. "Would you bring me a Mint Julep?" she asked the waiter. She did order lunch but not before she was on her third Mint Julep. She felt no pain. To use one of John's expressions: she was in "hog heaven"! Not surprisingly she was somewhat unsteady on her feet when we were ready to go; we had to take her by the arm and lead her to the car to take her home. Several days later we received the most eloquent letter in her beautiful script, thanking us profusely for the wonderful day we had given her.

The Elegant Bib also advertised with a free *dinner* when you turned 100. I'm sort of glad she didn't quite make it that far. But...every time I write the name Kuss I smile. So many memories! She definitely made our life more interesting.

CHAPTER 43

The Start of a Business

After the Oktoberfest with my German students I mentioned several chapters back, I began to explore the possibility of selling carnival supplies for school fundraisers in my spare time. I had been looking for a while for a part-time job in addition to teaching, which would make me eligible for Social Security later, a benefit denied to teachers.

Could I really make a profit? I wondered. I visited a few school carnivals, checking out what was needed for such an event: small toys, novelty items, stuffed animals, and rolls of tickets. From what I heard there was just one (franchised) supplier of that kind of merchandise in the area. Its owners usually didn't let PTA mothers pick and choose. Instead, they offered a package deal, more or less forcing the schools to take whatever prizes were offered. Improving on that concept seemed a no-brainer—let people in charge select their own merchandise and make prices slightly lower. My next step was finding a wholesaler or jobber of such goods.

Before the Internet was invented such a task took months of painstakingly checking lists provided by the national Chamber of Commerce, writing inquiries, and scouring price lists. In order to be competitive, I soon found that I *had* to buy at jobber's prices—below wholesale. That however, required buying in bulk, in case quantities. After many letters and phone calls a company named "Pico's" in Southern California sympathized with me. They let me buy in dozens and grosses at jobber's prices.

In June of 1973, on summer vacation from my full-time teaching job, I placed my first order for $500. We designated a small 4ft x 8ft room behind our garage as the "showroom," where John cleverly built page-like pegboard display units. Next I bought a calculator and blank invoices, and had an extra phone installed. The only thing left to do was finding customers.

Though John was always ready to help with anything I dreamed up, he didn't have much hope for the success of this new venture. He called it "Paula's little hobby." Joyce had already left home. Luke found it an unnecessary nuisance.

I sent flyers to all schools in the area and placed a small ad in the *Classified Flea Market*, a throwaway weekly. I worked *by appointment only*, after 3:00 p.m. daily.

I could have hugged my first customer, a woman ordering for a Danville school carnival to be held in October. It's funny how I *learned* from her and subsequent customers. They knew more about carnivals than I did! The Danville lady asked, "What kind of carnival games do you provide?" Gosh, I had seen games at the schools I visited but didn't know I was to make those available. "What would you like?" I bluffed. After writing down her list I promised to call her with their availability. She gave me a $300 order—10% down.

After she left I asked John, "Can you make a couple of tic-tac-toe and a seven-eleven games and a bean bag toss?" As John had visited various school carnivals with me he knew what I was talking about. I already owned one beanbag toss, made by one of my talented German students for the Oktoberfest: a huge caricature of Hitler with gaping mouth. I wasn't so sure how that would go over in conservative Danville.

Customers kept on coming—no one seemed to mind the long driveway and primitive showroom. By the end of the year, just three months after I welcomed my first customer, my sales totaled $18,000. "Pico's" received a lot more orders.

During December I realized there were other fundraisers to provide merchandise for, including school-organized Christmas bazaars, where students could buy inexpensive gifts for their families.

More unfamiliar requests poured in: "Do you have a wheel of fortune for rent?" (Or bingo cages, raffle drums.) Good heavens, where was I going to find all those things? I realized I needed to go to a trade show.

In January of 1974 I called in sick for a few days and flew to...Chicago! In order to gain entrance to this *general merchandise* show I had business cards printed with my name, address and the words: "Wholesale Supplies for Fundraising." The show was mind-boggling; a seemingly unending mass of booths manned by eager vendors. I had never seen so much merchandise together in one place. I ordered and ordered that first morning. In the afternoon, I did nothing but cancel. So many companies sold the same items that after some searching I found everything I originally bought at lower prices.

When I stood in front of my German class the day after my return I had to chuckle. *If you only knew where I spent the last few days....*

Not all my selections were fast sellers. Some of the gift items I liked received a cool reception. Even lowering the price didn't help. "I think I need to get a booth at a flea market," I told John. "Great, I'll get a bunch of junk together I've wanted to get rid of. Kill two birds with one stone," was his enthusiastic reply. The following Saturday we displayed our wares at a high school flea market with better results than expected. We set up shop at many more flea markets, raising much needed cash for new inventory. John loved to browse around other booths while I was selling. "Please don't get any new junk," I warned, after I saw him eyeing cast-offs at nearby booths.

New carnival requests started to come our way: "Can you supply *booths* and a *dunk tank?*" Realizing it was impossible to continue to teach full time I went on a part time schedule for two years and, after a total of ten years as a teacher, quit in 1977. John followed suit six months later.

In years to come, people gave *me* all the credit for starting the business. Yes, it had been my idea and I did all the buying and planning; but it was *John,* who did all the heavy work, building and organizing storage units in the garage, spending weeks cutting heavy, slotted iron into the right lengths to be made into booths. Each time these booths were rented out John had to load and unload them again. He did all the *behind the scenes* work. I can honestly say that without his help, the carnival business would never have gotten off the ground.

Yearly we provided goods for well over one hundred carnivals, close to fifty Christmas bazaars and numerous other fundraisers. Organizers of those events also bought a lot for themselves. They spread the word about all the gift items I had for sale at reduced prices. It always amused me when new customers called: "A friend of mine told me about your shop. Would you mind if I came over at 4:00 this afternoon...?" No, I didn't mind at all for someone to spend a few hundred bucks in my "store."

Together John and I attended several of the big merchandise shows all over the United States. Many of the exhibitors at those shows displayed the latest, hottest trends in general merchandise. In the mid seventies we noticed that an unusual number of merchants were offering dollhouse furniture for sale. Could that be the latest hobby? I took a chance and invested in a lot of miniature furniture as well as accessories like rugs, wallpaper, and even "families." When dollhouse mania started not long after, we were prepared. As an added dimension we had craftsmen make Victorian dollhouses for us, some selling for hundreds of dollars. It was not just a children's craze; women bought the more expensive version for their own collection. The trend lasted for years. As soon as it started to die out I held a big sale and completely sold out.

221

When the garage could no longer hold our ever-growing inventory we bought a used eight-by-twenty-foot cargo container. To make it look presentable John put siding on it to match the house, and put it next to the garage. After Luke left for college we changed both downstairs bedrooms into showrooms.

Where was this business heading? We felt we were pushing ourselves out of the house. In the midst of all this chaos, I received a call from someone organizing "home tours" as a fundraiser. "I heard you have such a lovely home. Do you think we could put it on our next tour?" Yeah, sure. We howled at the thought.

By the end of '78, after another successful carnival and Christmas season, I realized that, for this business to keep on growing, I would need people not only with energy and vision, but also with specific business knowledge to assist me. John tired easily and I knew full well I couldn't continue with my "by gosh and by golly" methods. To make matters worse, we received a letter from the county: "It has been brought to our attention that you are running a business from your home. As you reside in an area zoned "residential," such an operation is illegal. You are hereby ordered to quit within thirty days."

In the meantime, Luke had graduated from college with a business degree. After some discussion I offered him the job of store manager, as soon as he and his girlfriend—soon to be wife—returned from a post-graduate trip to Europe. As the business didn't earn a lot outside the fund-raising seasons, I could only offer Luke a modest starting salary.

Together Luke and I searched for a suitable, yet affordable business location. We settled on a newly-built warehouse in San Ramon—a ten-minute drive from our house. The price was right.

Since our new location had no walk-by traffic, there were many days—between carnival seasons—that we wondered if any customers would come. Luke went out on the road trying to sell to independent toy and gift shops, and any other businesses he felt might be interested in our items.

After a year of Luke's management, he and his wife came to the conclusion that they couldn't make ends meet on his earnings. They moved to San Diego, Mary Ellen's hometown.

That same year our only competitor in the area offered his entire carnival business for sale at a bargain price. Since it included a large inventory, a truck, and professionally made booth and games, it was too good a deal to pass up. But of course, it entailed a lot of extra work. We hired a warehouse manager for all the heavy work, as well as two part-time female employees. The business really started to take off. We began to realize how much Luke's management had contributed to the successful operation of the store, and wished he were back.

In 1981 Mary Ellen gave birth to our first grandchild, Emily. What should have been a period of great joy became a time of worry and deep concern about Emily's health; she was born with several very serious congenital heart defects. Although both Luke and Mary Ellen had medical insurance through their employers, they were still responsible for the skyrocketing co-pay. With no relief in sight for them, I decided to make Luke another offer with a dual purpose: to get the right help for Emily and have the three of them move back to the Bay Area. Luke was to become an equal partner in the business, splitting everything 50-50, in exchange for working full time for Boswell's. Included in the deal was a group medical plan that covered all expenses regarding Emily's health.

Though we already had a thriving business going, Luke and Mary Ellen both had a broader vision of what Boswell's could become. They immediately started to stock party supplies as an important part of the store's product mix. They purchased attractive used store fixtures—a vast improvement over the conglomeration of display cases we had accumulated over the years. Walls of the warehouse were removed, doubling the size of the store.

As Mary Ellen believed that multiple locations would make Boswell's more viable and competitive, she became the driving force behind opening three more stores in the next few years: one in Lafayette, then Pleasanton, followed by a fourth one in Concord.

John and I seriously assessed the situation. Though we were happy that Luke and Mary Ellen had the desire and energy to expand, *we* wanted to take it easier. John's health in particular made it hard for him to be involved at all. He much preferred to stay home, writing or puttering in the yard. So we made the decision to sell the majority of our share. As part of the buy-out we were given sole ownership of the—still rather small—Lafayette store. Several times over the years I moved it to a more visible and larger location. As John and I liked to spend a lot of time together, whether at home or on trips, I hired enough capable employees to run it without my being there every day.

On January 1, 2000, the first day of the new millennium, I called it quits, selling our last interest in the business to our son and daughter-in-law. They still own and operate all four stores. Though fundraisers remained an important part of their business for several years, the focus in the stores became *party supplies.* Carnivals in most schools were replaced with more lucrative fundraisers, like auctions.

As for Emily, with the availability of a top-notch surgeon provided through their HMO, she underwent successful open-heart surgery when she was two years old. This enabled her to lead a fairly normal life.

CHAPTER 44

Our Church Life

Though my parents, like the majority of the Dutch, weren't overly religious, they were good, law-abiding citizens. They did believe in a God but, with the exception of the times we were baptized, rarely attended church. However, they felt it was their parental duty to expose us kids to the teachings of the Bible. From the time I was six until I turned twelve, I attended Sunday school at a nearby church, together with my siblings. Each time we were given five pennies for the collection box. As it happened, our walk to this weekly event took us right past a candy store. I must shamefully confess, that two of my five pennies never reached their rightful destination.

John had told me that his immediate family was Methodist and that his father had been a devout Christian, who prayed daily. One of John's brothers mentioned much later how their father would seclude himself from the rest of the family to *talk to God*. While John was in prison camp his dad prayed for his safe return. One day, after such a session, he rejoined the family and told them he had gotten a message: "Ray will return alive but I won't be here anymore to witness it."

When we moved to Beaufort SC in 1954 John was happy to find a Methodist church we could attend. I wasn't all that anxious to go but told John I'd give it a try.

What a surprise was waiting for me! How different church life was in the States!

In Holland the (few) church services I had attended were just that: a one-hour service with a sermon and a few hymns. There was absolutely no other church life, no social get-togethers, no committees, no *nothing*.

The very first Sunday we attended the Beaufort Methodist Church we were made truly welcome. Other parishioners seemed genuinely pleased we came and invited us to a *Young Couples* group afterwards. Joyce went to Sunday school and Luke stayed in a well-run nursery.

I soon became an enthusiastic churchgoer. Together we joined many of their social groups and committees. I also played the piano for a Sunday school class. After a while I was asked to be part of a group that performed for a radio program. My first "assignment" was reading the St. Francis of Assisi prayer to a radio audience. I had never heard the prayer before and it made a deep impression on me. For his 34th birthday I gave John a bible.

When we moved to Pleasant Hill, CA in 1956, we started to attend the Walnut Creek Methodist Church. We immediately felt very much at home and soon became members. We had wonderful experiences at that church, made many friends, and served in a lot of functions, sometimes as greeters or serving coffee, teaching Sunday school, or helping out in the office. We participated in many social activities as well. Our children sang in a choir and became involved in youth groups when they reached a certain age.

Each time my mother visited from Holland she attended church with us. She loved the churches in the States so much that she applied for membership in one of the few American churches that happened to be in The Hague.

After moving to Danville in '69 we felt we should be attending the Methodist Church in the Alamo/Danville area. We transferred our membership and once again became active. Dr Grey, the minister at that time, was an outstanding speaker. His sermons carried inspiring and thought-provoking messages. I wrote my mother about several of his sermons that had a real impact on me. In one sermon he quoted the poem:

A bell is no bell till you ring it
A song is no song till you sing it
And love was not put in your heart there to stay
Love is not love till you give it away.

I thought about that last sentence for a long time. Had I made any progress as a Christian since Toto's death four years earlier? Had I made any changes in my life, as I had promised myself I would? Had I consciously made an effort to think about and do something for people outside my family? I had to admit I probably had changed a little but there was still a lot of room for improvement. Why couldn't I be more like John, who did so much for others? I vowed again that I would try harder.

About a year after becoming members we were asked to be part of a committee on *social concerns*. This was at the time when Joyce had a serious drug problem. The committee discussed what the church could do for its young people. John and I suggested making a space available where the teenagers could meet and possibly get some counseling for drug and alcohol problems.

Several members were aghast. "Teenagers in the Danville and Alamo area don't have those problems," they proclaimed. We couldn't believe what we heard. To deny this very serious problem in our valley was something we simply couldn't accept. It was just too hypocritical. Wasn't the church there to help others in need? We quit going to church. Maybe not the best solution but at the time we felt we couldn't in good conscious continue.

About six years later, during one of my mother's visits, she asked, "Would you mind going with me to your old church in Walnut Creek one time?" The two of us did just that the following Sunday. I hadn't anticipated that it would feel so good going back. Our old friends welcomed us like long lost relatives. Moreover, their new minister, Doug Hayward, delivered dynamic sermons. They contained messages we discussed for days. It also felt great to hear wonderful choir music again. Soon John joined us and got the same warm reception. And so we went back and became active members again.

Many years later, after Dr. Hayward's retirement, a new minister was appointed. In deference to his family and friends I'll refer to him as "Ken White"—not his real name. He was in his mid fifties. His wife's ancestors came from Germany.

On February 26, 1989, Ken preached a sermon, titled: "Kindling the Non-Consuming Fires." It dealt with Moses in the desert and how God used "a flame of fire out of the midst of a bush" to get his attention. The minister then asked, "Is there 'a flame of fire' that has ever caught our attention?"

To our utter disbelief he gave as examples: "Two compelling February 1945 horrors, one in Germany and the other in Tokyo," the fire bombings by the Allied Forces that caused much destruction and loss of lives.

I was aghast. Didn't he know who started the war? Didn't he remember what the Germans did to the Jews? The deaths and destruction in Holland? And above all, the indescribable horrors John had endured in Japanese POW camps flashed through my mind. I looked at John who was also visibly shaken. "Do you want to leave?" he asked. Together we walked out of the church.

A few days later, not unexpectedly, we received a call from Ken: "Can I come and see you? I think we should talk." We set a date and time. John had his speech ready. He was going to point out that the Allies' task had been to defeat a monster; make the minister realize that without our military aggression we would all be speaking German or Japanese today. However, the discussion took a different direction.

When Reverend White arrived we invited him to sit down, awaiting his explanation. Ken started: "You have to understand that I was just a little boy during WWII. I didn't know much about what was happening." John's obvious question to this remark was, "Why talk about something you are unfamiliar with?" Then he asked the minister if he would like to borrow some books that gave an overview of all that happened. Ken answered, "I'm a very busy man; I really don't have time to read." After a moment of silence John said, "If that's the case I think it's a waste of time to discuss this matter further."

We never went back to church. It wasn't that we were *un*religious. John, in particular, often prayed for his departed family and buddies. We started to listen to Sunday morning worship services on TV.

I had driven by our old church in Alamo numerous times without giving it any thought. About six months after John died, in spite of the help from my family and support groups, I still had a hard time coping with the realization that our life together on earth was over.

The next time I drove by that church I suddenly felt a pull, like a magnet. I attended church the following Sunday and knew that I had "come home." I felt not only God's presence but John's as well. I knew he would be happy with my decision.

CHAPTER 45

Heart Attack!

On February 28, 1977, the day before our twenty-fifth wedding anniversary I wrote my mother: *I'm so excited about tomorrow. I don't think John and I have ever been as happy as we are right now. I hope we'll have each other for many more years.*

Luke called us from San Diego, wishing us a Happy Anniversary. He said, "I really appreciate that you have such a solid marriage. So many of my friends' parents are divorced. Your togetherness has contributed to my being so well adjusted." He couldn't have given us a nicer present.

A year later we reached another milestone: we both retired from teaching. We still had our very busy home business, but that was conducted strictly on our own time, and at our own pace. It was exhilarating! No more alarm clock for us, no more commute, no homework to correct, nor lesson plans to make.

In May we survived another carnival season and saw our son graduate from college. On June 25, I wrote my mother: *Though our life is very busy, we enjoy all the little things we do together. Our life is so good, that once in a while I can't help but think what it would be like if John were no longer with me.*

Two days later John suffered a massive heart attack. The previous day he had been working in the yard, the kind of strenuous work he enjoyed. He always claimed that working outdoors made him feel better physically. At one point though, he stumbled inside, complaining about mild chest pains. The next day he went on an errand with a friend. I received a phone call twenty minutes later: "You better come and pick John up, he's in terrible pain; I think he may have had a heart attack."

I rushed right over. As John's pain had subsided somewhat he insisted, "Let's go home; I'm really tired." "No way," I replied, "we're going to the emergency room." I was thinking of John's brother T.B., who had not been able to get medical help fast enough after a heart attack and had died at age forty-five. Getting John to a doctor quickly was a matter of life or death in my mind. Luckily, we were only five minutes from the nearest hospital.

He was admitted at once. Shortly after they hooked him up to an IV and several monitors, John suffered a second, much more severe attack, sending him into shock. He spent the next two weeks in the ICU.

My heart ached each time I visited, seeing him lie there, connected to a multitude of tubes and monitors. Even with all the morphine the doctors administered he was in a lot of pain and didn't want to see anyone but me.

We were all relieved to hear that the doctors were cautiously optimistic. Since John had come to the hospital well within that first critical "golden" hour, bypass surgery remained an option in the future.

Several weeks later he was declared well enough to continue his recuperation at home. It shocked me to see how frail he looked. The powerful pain medications made him listless and drowsy.

As was to be expected, he was put on severe restrictions. His diet was changed dramatically; instead of big pieces of carrot cake and half-gallons of ice cream he was allowed only healthy food with little salt and fat. As far as limiting his activities was concerned, he wasn't even able to walk more than a few steps. Reading a book was too much. But hey, we were grateful he was *alive!* Yes, alive, but extremely weak for months.

Everybody was very concerned; many prayers were sent his way. Our children and friends came over regularly to keep him company and entertain him. Having work to do, I couldn't sit by his side the entire day, so I invited his brother Jake for a visit. Very slowly, John started to regain some strength. Real strenuous work was out of the question forever; we sold the wheelbarrow, cement mixer, weed eater, and other, now unused equipment.

Two months later another carnival season started. John, worried that it would be too much work for me to do alone, offered to help me pack orders. I quickly declined his offer: "Remember what the doctor told you; you're not supposed to do any lifting and reaching." That's when John came up with a great idea: "Then I'm going to help you in the house. I'll make breakfast every morning and keep the kitchen clean." Never having liked kitchen work I gratefully accepted his offer.

Oh, how I relished that new daily routine! Up at around 8:00. After getting dressed I sat down in my recliner, waiting to be spoiled. (We always ate breakfast on trays in the living room.) John was up to the task he himself had suggested. He was much better at it than I, keeping a spotless kitchen. Before making breakfast he would get me the newspaper, which required a drive to the bottom of the hill. Breakfast usually consisted of cereal with strawberries and a glass of fresh-squeezed orange juice. Whenever I heard the whirring of the juicer I felt content with my life. After so many months filled with concern about John's health we were still together, sharing the good life again.

I have to confess at this point, that John's taking care of the kitchen had its irritating moments. He was such a perfectionist, so organized, that at times I got "called in" for a *misdeed*. Whenever he yelled, "Paula," in a reprimanding voice, I knew I had done something wrong. I may have put a fork in the dishwasher with the *tines up*, or put a tea bag in the disposal. I did not want to complain about his reactions to such trivial matters; I was just happy he did so much housework for me.

Before my first daily customers were scheduled we had enough time set aside to go into town for a cup of coffee at Father Nature's, our favorite café.

The following year John felt well enough to accompany me again to trade shows: Las Vegas, Chicago, Los Angeles, or anywhere else I wanted to go. We stayed at hotels adjacent to the shows, which enabled him to go back to the room whenever he became weary. We always managed to combine such a trip with a vacation, eating in nice restaurants and doing a little gambling. John wasn't much of a gambler. After feeding a few rolls of quarters into a machine he usually called it quits. That's why it came as a big surprise he once hit a $7000 jackpot on a quarter slot machine! The payout came of course with an income tax form, but who cared? It was still a lot of money.

When time permitted we traveled to foreign destinations, which led us to Rio de Janeiro in 1984. With the sweltering temperature combined with high humidity John started to have breathing problems. On our return we were told his heart needed "repairs": bypass surgery. While on the operating table he suffered another heart attack, which made the surgery more complex and recuperation longer. My dear husband worried, not about his own condition but about *me*; that it may be too strenuous for me to make the daily trips to visit him in the San Francisco hospital. At times I wondered if I deserved such an unselfish, loving man.

John was elated to get home from the hospital. Soon he started to paddle around in the pool. With the temperature at a warm 90 degrees we frequently swam early in the morning, and floated around in the moonlight in the evenings.

Before we went to Holland the following year my mother, concerned about John's health, asked me about his diet, what kind of restrictions he was on. "Tell her I'm on a *stroopwafel* diet," was John's joking reply. He never lost his love for those Dutch cookies.

233

As for his heart, with the help of several gadgets and procedures: rotoblading, stents, angioplasty, and pacemaker it served him for twenty-five more years from the time of his first heart attack.

John and his brother Jake

CHAPTER 46

Once a Marine Always a Marine

During his last year in the service (1956 – 1957), John was invited once again to become an officer. Had he accepted— and been able to pass the physical this time—he couldn't possibly have retired in August of 1957. Going to college was first and foremost on his mind. Waiting another few years would only have made it more difficult. So he declined. On August 31, 1957, twenty years and eleven days after enlisting in the Marine Corps, John returned to civilian life.

"There's no such thing as an ex-Marine," John often said. However, during almost two decades after retirement he needed to "take a breather" from the Corps, to heal from the mental wounds still open from his POW years. One of his friends continued to write letters to "MSgt John Boswell Ret." It annoyed John. "I am a civilian now, leave the title off please," he wrote back.

This all changed with the start of POW reunions in the mid seventies, getting together with survivors of the old "China Marines," the 4th Regiment. Not all survivors wanted to attend these reunions—many still found it too painful to talk about their horrific experiences.

John understood those feelings well. When he received word about the first reunion he had mixed emotions and decided not to go; he had finally come to terms with what had happened during his years as a POW, and had tried to erase those agonizing memories from his mind.

In 1976 the China Marine's reunion was held in Albuquerque NM, the city his cousin Chuck, as well as his good friend Siegfried Hahn had moved to years ago. Siegfried had made quite a name for himself as artist and teacher. "Why don't we go together?" John suggested. "After visiting with Chuck and Siegfried we'll stop by the reunion site."

Though pleased to see some of his old China Marine friends, John felt it sat him back emotionally, reliving those horror years. For a while he wished he had stayed home. During the following year however, he received several letters from his POW friends telling him how pleased they had been to see him and urging him to come again.

When a reunion was announced a year later in San Diego, where Luke was attending college, he said to his son, "Come with me to the Marine reunion. If I don't see anybody I know, we'll do something else together." Luke told me later, that the moment his dad entered the reunion hall, he was surrounded by old friends. "John, is that you?" someone shouted. It was Bob Martineau, who had lost a leg fighting on Corregidor. Luke was forgotten. From then on John became an enthusiastic reunion visitor.

About two hundred men attended the reunions in the early years. Not bad, considering that of the original 750 men in the 4th Marine Regiment only around 450 had survived prison camp. By 2003, John's last year of attendance, there were less than thirty left.

It brought comfort to the men to be in the company of former POWs, who shared a common understanding of the horrors they had endured. They encouraged each other to "let it all out"; it was okay to be angry. They compared their experiences with the Veterans Administration and imparted information on claims, and pensions due ex-POWs with serious health problems. Last but not least, their gatherings made them realize, that their stories *had* to be told to the rest of the world.

In the following years many books were written about life in Japanese prison camps. Several of the men—John included—started to give talks to schools, service clubs, and any other groups that were interested in hearing about the POWs' experience.

During one reunion a list was made available of all Marines from the old 4th Regiment who were still alive. To John's delight he found a few living in the Bay Area who for one reason or another, had chosen not to attend the yearly meetings. John called them after returning home.

Soon that little group: four former POWs plus their Shanghai CO, who had been lucky enough to take the last boat out of China, started to meet weekly. Once a month the wives were invited. It became routine to have a big Marine Corps Birthday party each year on November 10.

In 1990, John joined a group of POW survivors going to the Philippines to visit what was left of the various prison camps. John re-visited the ruins of Middleside barracks on Corregidor and flew to Palawan Island, landing on the airstrip he and his fellow-prisoners had been forced to help build as slave laborers. Though a very emotional experience, it was a trip he had wanted to take for a long time.

The U.S. Government was not the swiftest with issuing well-deserved medals. In 1988 a ceremony was held at San Francisco's Presidio Army Base, where prison camp survivors were issued their POW medals. In '92 John and the rest of the China Marines were awarded the Bronze Star Medal for fighting on Corregidor exactly fifty years before. When John became aware he was entitled to a Purple Heart medal he applied and received that as well. With all his ailments, originating during his imprisonment, John received a 100% disability rating from the VA in 1992.

Aside from his many speaking engagements John started to do a lot of writing. "You ought to write a book," was the frequently heard request from friends. Though he felt enough books had already been written on the subject, he often wrote out page after page in longhand as well as on an old typewriter. He never felt comfortable with the computer or word processor Luke had bought him.

Being one of the few POWs left in the area John was often interviewed. Many articles and pictures appeared in local newspapers. In January '92, after an account about his experiences, the writer added, "Former Marine John Boswell of Danville looks fit enough to whip a bunch of recruits into shape." After a talk to veterans in the Rossmoor Retirement community in March '97, an article stated, "John Boswell appeared as perky as a spring robin except for a few maladies common to senior citizens." "I wished I felt that fit and perky," John sighed after reading those comments.

The Contra Costa Times of June 18, 2000, wrote, "Boswell, who has visited classrooms to share his war experiences, has a library in his Danville home with more WWII material than one could read in a lifetime." Over the years John had gone from second-hand bookstores, to antique bookstores, to garage sales, and flea markets to search for books on the war in the Pacific.

I personally found John's talks to groups on his experiences more interesting when he first started giving them. The more often he talked about his life as a POW, the more incensed he became at the Japanese government for never having shown the slightest remorse for the dismal conduct of the military: their brutalities, their executions, and beheadings for no reason at all. "They justified their behavior by saying they strictly adhered to the 'Bushido' code, the code of the warrior. They took everything away from me: my freedom, my dignity, food and health," he often mentioned. "Red Cross packages, meant for the POWs, which could have saved thousands of lives, were found stacked up high in Japanese warehouses after the war."

He always explained at the beginning of his talks, "I'm not speaking about the Japanese *civilians*, many of whom are good and decent people. I'm talking about the Japanese military, the *Bushido boys*." In spite of that caveat he got some flack. After a speech to a group of survivors of the Battle of the Bulge, a Japanese woman stood up and demanded an apology from John for what he had said about her countrymen. "Lady," John answered, trying not to show his anger, "I'm only telling the *truth*. If you can't take that, that's your problem."

John's audiences often called him a *hero*. He denied that praise. "I'm not a *hero*, I'm a *survivor*."

John showing his medals and ribbons during an interview

At a China Marine reunion

CHAPTER 47

The Veterans of San Ramon Valley

The get-togethers of the small group of POWs living in the Bay Area continued for many years. Inevitably, one after the other died. By the mid-nineties John was the only one still alive. As the weekly meetings with his old friends had become an important part of John's life, the deaths of these men created a vacuum, an emptiness in him.

As luck would have it he ran into a Navy veteran. "You ought to come to the veterans' coffee," he suggested. Unbeknownst to John, a group of veterans from every branch of the service, ranking from PFC to general and admiral, met each morning from 10 till 11 at the "Rising Loafer," a Danville coffee shop.

John decided to see what the meetings were all about. After just one visit he came home enthusiastically: "What a great bunch of guys! I wished I'd known about them years ago." Though he didn't mention it, I'm sure he was happy to have a new audience for his jokes.

The veterans welcomed him with open arms. As the only ex-POW, his stories added a new dimension to the group. Not that the other attendees didn't have interesting experiences—far from it. One Marine survived the battles of Iwo Jima; another had seen action in Germany as a bomber pilot, and a third had served on an aircraft carrier in the Pacific. Several of the men had fought in Vietnam and Korea. It truly was a unique bunch of aging veterans gathering for coffee five times a week.

With so many fascinating stories ready to be told, John came up with a plan: "Why don't we contact local high schools and colleges? We can offer to tell our stories to history and social science classes." After the veterans all agreed to take part in this effort John made up a roster, listing everyone's expertise, including their theater of action.

For a while all went according to plan. Usually two veterans talked during one class session. Students seemed to thoroughly enjoy getting this first-hand knowledge.

However, at one high school—I won't mention names— the principal informed them that they needed permission from the school district superintendent to continue with their talks. Soon an appointment was made to that effect. John and two other veterans went to the district offices for a meeting. After waiting for a while the men were told, "Sorry, the superintendent is all tied up; why don't you come back another time?" A second appointment was set up with more or less the same result. A third attempt was made: "I'll get back to you," they were told. That's when John said, "Guys, we're wasting our time. It's obvious they don't want us."

I well remember John's frustration over this issue: "Sugarcoating the brutality," he called it, "whitewashing history."

Reflecting on that refusal now, more than ten years later, it still boggles my mind. Didn't that superintendent realize what he was denying the students in his district? To hear those fascinating stories *first hand* about battles and survival sixty years earlier from veterans of the "Greatest Generation," who were dying off at a rate of fifteen hundred per day? What a truly rare opportunity was missed for thousands of young people to see history come alive. Fortunately there were other school districts and organizations eager to hear the unique stories told by John and his fellow veterans.

Before long John was asked to join several veterans' organizations. He became a member of the Veterans of Foreign Wars (VFW), Marine Corps League, and the American Legion, to name a few. With their combined meetings he became a busy man.

In addition to the magazines he already subscribed to, like the "Leatherneck," the official Marine Corps magazine, John started to receive periodicals from the new service clubs he had joined. While he loved to read those military publications it brought unexpected headaches for the family and me. Handguns and shotguns were advertised in abundance. Though we had an elaborate alarm system in our home, John often remarked, "We should have a gun in the house to protect ourselves." No matter how much Luke and I argued that it was too dangerous, especially with the grandchildren around, he insisted on buying several pistols at a local gun shop. When Luke threatened not to let the children visit anymore, John agreed to keep them in gun boxes with safety locks. After John's death Luke donated them all to the local police.

Guns were not the only things John noticed in the military magazines. Clothing was offered at low prices. John's taste in clothes had never been great, a fact he didn't deny. "You can pick and choose for me," he told me early on. Now suddenly packages arrived from "Haband" men's furnishings. The cheapest looking pants appeared and, Good Lord Almighty, I thought, tennis *shoes with Velcro straps.* While little kids' shoes with Velcro looked cute, a size twelve man's shoe was something else. I wanted my husband to look "sharp," not nerdy. The pants could be used for yard work but the shoes *had to go!* After some muttering: "You know, at times you can be a real pain in the neck," he agreed to send the shoes back.

Not long after John's death I had coffee with the veterans group. In walked the admiral, *with the identical Velcro tennis shoes* I had so detested. Yes John, I admitted finally, I really had been too picky. In the greater scheme of things what would it have mattered?

The local veterans played an important part in the remaining years of John's life. Through their efforts a flag was flown over the U.S. Capitol on September 2, 1997 in his honor. At a special ceremony John received that flag together with a certificate stating:

This flag was flown for Master Sergeant John R. Boswell, U.S. Marine Corps, Retired, to commemorate the surrender of the Imperial Japanese Government and the liberation of Marine John R. Boswell from POW camps in September, 1945.

More honors followed after his death.

In front of the Rising Loafer

With his veteran friends at a VFW meeting

CHAPTER 48

Forty Years of Marriage

Doubting if John, with all his ailments, would be able to make it till our fiftieth wedding anniversary, we threw a big bash for our fortieth in 1992. The year before, we had added a bonus room to our house, which made it easier to host a large group of guests. Joyce, together with a niece who had recently moved to the San Francisco Peninsula, was in charge of entertainment.

John almost missed his own party. At 5:00 p.m., less than an hour before friends and relatives were to arrive he had one of his "episodes," as his doctors called it. He suddenly turned ashen, started to sweat profusely and had difficulty breathing. What to do? It was too late to call off the whole party as the caterers would be arriving soon with dinner for forty-five people. But we knew John needed help. Joyce offered to take him to the emergency room at John Muir Hospital.

Everyone obviously was surprised and concerned when they heard what happened. Joyce called me several times, keeping us informed. After she had explained the circumstances to the staff at the hospital, John was tended to at once. A little after seven o'clock she phoned with the joyful news that her dad was ready to be released. Just as we were about to sit down to dinner John made his grand entrance to a cheering crowd. After a bad beginning the party became a big success.

The following day, relaxing after that event, we started to reminisce about our forty years of marriage. Why had we succeeded while several couples we knew had split up? We both felt that there had to be love of course, but also mutual respect and a sharing of interests. There were many similarities in our likes and dislikes. First and foremost we shared our great love for our children and grandchildren.

We touched upon Joyce's teenage years. Yes, they had been exasperating at times, especially during her "hippy" escapades. After searching for deeper meaning in her life, which had led to some bad decisions, she turned her life around and became a committed Christian. Regrettably, her marriage to Charles in 1981 ended in divorce seven years later. They had no children.

During her hippy years Joyce had dropped out of college. John and I were both thrilled when she resumed her studies and got her degree while she was in her late thirties. An excellent job at Kaiser Permanente was the result.

As for our son Luke, his life had followed a more traditional path. John and Luke had shared many good times together: participating in the Indian Guides as a father/son team, and in the seventies attending numerous Oakland Raider games during the Raiders' glory years.

While in college Luke met his future wife Mary Ellen and by now had four children. We were grateful Emily, in spite of her heart condition, was doing well. Next came Megan, one year younger, followed in 1988 by Martine, and last but not least Dalton in 1990.

Those four grandchildren truly made our life complete. Living just five minutes from our house we were their home away from home. All four loved to stay with their Oma and Opa. They were always eager to be entertained. "Opa, get your guitar, let's sing some silly songs." Or, "Opa, tell us a sea story." Another request: "Opa, swear in Japanese." John was only too happy to comply, teaching them new songs, inventing long tales and uttering what was supposed to be a Japanese swear word: "sanamekawallakapeewa."

Next they would turn to me: "Oma, do you have any junk food?" That's not exactly what I fed them, but as their parents adhered to a very strict, healthy food regimen, our ordinary food tasted rich and sinful to them.

Suffice it to say, that foursome brought us a lot of happiness. We sincerely hoped to have many more enjoyable years with them.

We shared quite a few other interests besides our family. All the traveling we had done. We could have talked about those journeys alone for days on end. On one of our most recent trips we had visited Edinburgh, Scotland, searching for records on John's forefathers, trying to find out when they emigrated to the U.S. We had been frustrated to learn that record-keeping didn't start until 1845, just a few years after a group of Boswells had left Scotland. The discovery of a tiny town named St. Boswells a few days later made up for that disappointment.

Yet, even though traveling was one of our favorite pastimes, we were also perfectly happy to be home together, sharing our afternoon cup of tea—always with a treat. I must confess that we were both gluttons when it came to sweets.

We thought of the business trips to San Francisco we made in our van, picking up merchandise from vendors. Invariably our first stop was the "Swedish," the—now defunct—bakery on Powell Street that I have mentioned before. They made many pastries filled with thick layers of almond paste, my absolute favorite treat. Whenever the three pastries I liked best were available, I shamefully admit I ate one of each! Once when I was on a diet (an oft-recurring event) a friend asked me, "Do you eat just *one* pastry now?" "No," I replied, "I eat two instead of three." John was almost as bad as I was.

The fact that neither of us grew up in luxury made us doubly appreciate all we had accomplished in our life. Last but not least, we gave each other a lot of freedom—we trusted each other completely. That reality alone contributed much to the success of our marriage.

Sure, we had our little disagreements and occasionally would get irritated or impatient with each other. We didn't always agree on TV programs to watch. An entire day of football was a little more than I could stand. And whenever John wanted to watch *boxing*, I made a hasty retreat to the bonus room.

Though grudgingly at times, we tolerated each other's whims. While it may seem I had more zany ideas than John, he had his share of quirks as well. I remember one case in particular: While planning a European vacation with our children, John insisted we take a "side trip" from Stockholm to Helsinki to...shake the hand of a *Finn*, as he wanted to thank Finland for being the only country that had paid back their war debt to the U.S. "Can't we just go to the Finnish Consulate in San Francisco to find a Finn?" I feebly suggested. No, it had to be a Finn on his own soil. As a trip on a ferry would have taken sixteen hours one way, we went by plane, stayed one day and one night before flying back. In my opinion an extremely expensive (and unnecessary) handshake. But hey, it made him one happy guy.

Now that we had reached this milestone of forty years, we started to wonder what else was in store for us in the coming years. How much longer would we be allowed to be together? Could we dare hope to still have each other ten years from now? We decided to take it day by day, enjoying each moment.

Joyce as a twelve year old with her mom

The family during the children's teenage years

At Paula and John's 30th wedding anniversary

Megan (left) and Emily with their Opa and Oma

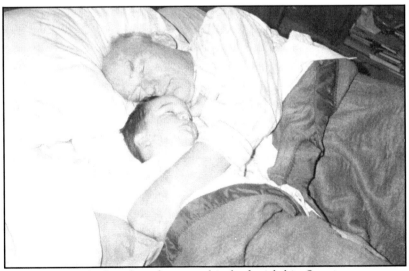

Dalton loved to crawl in bed with his Opa

Watching a funny program with Martine

CHAPTER 49

The New Millennium

With the ringing in of the New Year on January 1, 2000, we gave each other a big hug and said, "Can you believe it? We made it!" What we marveled at was the fact John had actually managed to survive to the new millennium, a feat we had never expected years ago. We received a letter from one of his China Marine friends, echoing the same sentiment: "Who, in their wildest dreams, could have predicted fifty-five years ago that we would be here today to celebrate the beginning of the new century?"

The next day, my seventy-fifth birthday, we sold our last interest in the party business—the store in Lafayette—to Luke and Mary Ellen. Though for many years I had worked only four or five hours a day and taken long vacations, it was a relief to be completely free from the hassle associated with operating a retail store.

John's health was our biggest concern now. His cardiologist had tried several times to restore John's irregular heart beat (atrial fibrillation) with minimal results. Though new medications became available, John's body didn't tolerate them. By now his health had deteriorated to the stage where visits to many specialists became routine. Most of his ailments: heart disease, lung and kidney problems, and skin cancers were attributed to his prison camp years. Like many people his age he also suffered from arthritis. As I wanted to hear first-hand what was wrong I accompanied him to all of his appointments.

John's physical therapist had repeatedly told him a *walking cane* would give a lot of support. Reluctant at first ("I'd *really* feel like an old man") he agreed to take a look in a cane store in Pleasanton. When he saw one with a fancy, simulated marble, form-fitted handle, he relented. It became his constant companion.

We were lucky *my* health remained good. Just a few hip replacements and shoulder surgery—all repairable problems. John, glad to repay me for my devotion to him during his many ailments, made my hospital stays almost bearable. At eight in the morning, ignoring any hospital rules about visiting hours, he would bring me fresh-squeezed orange juice and, if I'd let him, would have stayed all day.

How I wished that John's medical troubles were as easy to fix as mine. Yet, he rarely complained. On the contrary, he always remained upbeat. Though he couldn't possibly have felt that great, it didn't prevent him from having a good time with his grandchildren, lunches with Luke, outings with Joyce, traveling together, and visiting with the veterans in Danville. When he could no longer drive, I took him to the coffee group in the morning, picking him up later. Often we would continue on to have lunch somewhere. Every Saturday morning we had breakfast at Father Nature's. John also did a lot of writing, corresponding with old POW friends and jotting down his memories from the war years.

Trips to San Francisco became less frequent. However, when a popular musical came to town, we would take *BART* (rapid transit) into the city, have lunch, and attend a matinee performance. The very last musical we saw was "Mamma Mia."

Over the years we had taken all our grandchildren—one or two at a time—on extended trips, often to foreign destinations. Some of those journeys resulted in unforgettable experiences, like the time when we took eleven year-old Emily with us on a Danube cruise.

We had arrived in Vienna, our starting point, a few days early. One afternoon, coming down from our room at the Hotel Intercontinental, we noticed a lot of commotion in the lobby. Looking closer we saw this man in his flowing pink robes, with a large entourage, walking by: The *DALAI LAMA!* When he saw Emily he suddenly stopped, walked towards her and hugged her, saying, "Bless you, my child." The whole incident took just a few moments but it left a deep impression on the three of us, Emily in particular.

Our son asked us on return, "Did you take a picture?" We laughed. Sure Luke, we should have grabbed this world-renowned spiritual leader by the arm and said, "Wait a minute, sir, would you hug her again, so we can immortalize the moment?"

Cruising had long since become our favorite way of travel. As long as John assured me he could manage those trips, I kept looking for new exciting destinations.

The year 2001 started with a cruise around South America, followed by one to Alaska in July. Between those two voyages we attended a China Marine reunion in St. Louis, and visited Bonifay again.

In August we drove for four days up the coast to Mendocino, Joyce's—early—gift to us for our fiftieth wedding anniversary. Afraid her dad may not make it till the actual date of March 1, 2002, she decided to organize the trip seven months early. John did remarkably well on all those outings. Best of all, he truly enjoyed them.

By the end of the year, John's cardiologist decided it was time for a pacemaker/defibrillator to prevent his heart from going haywire.

John had always loved a glass (or two) of wine with dinner. When I expressed concern to his doctor, wondering how much harm that may cause, considering his health problems and all the medications he was taking, the doctor answered, "At his age, let him have that little pleasure."

257

To me, that sounded alarmingly like, "He isn't going to last much longer anyway." The worst was yet to come.

On a South American cruise—February 2001

July 2001—Alaskan cruise

CHAPTER 50

The Final Years

Shortly after John received a pacemaker for his atrial fibrillation in December of 2001, I observed a few disturbing changes in him. "Why did you change the channel?" he would ask each time a commercial cut into a TV program. He became much more forgetful, which he attributed to his "rice brain" as he called it—eating only rice as a POW. Time-related questions puzzled him. He thought the year was 1989 and couldn't remember the name of the president.

At first I hoped his many medications were the culprit. A specially designed test for detecting early dementia proved otherwise—he was diagnosed as being in the early stages of Alzheimer's disease. "Aricept" was added to his list of pills.

For the family and me this was devastating news. It wasn't what we had wanted for John's last years on this earth. Moreover, he didn't want to accept the diagnosis: "I don't have Alzheimer's; I'm just getting more forgetful," he said after hearing the test results. His refusal to accept the inevitable made the situation more difficult for me. I could have helped him make decisions for the future when he would no longer be able to make rational choices.

During the previous summer, just in the nick of time, Luke made a video of John, talking about Bonifay and prison camp. To keep the stories in sequence, Luke posed the questions, to which John provided the answers. The whole video was several hours long.

We didn't get to see it until the spring of 2002. John looked at it intently and exclaimed, "I couldn't agree more with what that guy is saying. That's exactly how I feel!" He didn't know he was looking at his own image.

For months there was no change in John's daily morning routine; unaided he continued to take long showers, and had no difficulty getting dressed. Just before ten o'clock I'd take him to the coffee group. Even the veterans didn't realize his true condition. As they told me later, they thought he was just getting more forgetful. His confusion usually started later in the day; it's called *sundowning.*

For our fiftieth wedding anniversary we flew to Kauai for a week. John seemed to thoroughly enjoy the vacation. Other than getting lost trying to find the hotel room he did remarkably well.

In the summer of 2002 we re-visited Holland and Portugal, and in the fall of the same year took a Pacific Island cruise. This was a cruise for veterans, visiting islands where battles had been fought in WWII, like Midway, Guam, Saipan, Guadalcanal and Iwo Jima. John, being the only POW survivor present, often was the center of attention.

We made one more trip to Bonifay in April of 2003. His brother Jake was in much worse shape mentally than John and told the wildest stories. I remember after one such tale John was still alert enough to say, "Jake, that's the biggest bunch of bullshit I've heard in a long time."

John, as always, was happy to visit Bonifay again. On the first night, after arriving at a nearby motel, he gave me a big hug and said, "Have I told you lately that you are the most wonderful woman in the world and that I love you very much?" I was so exhausted after driving for five hours that all I could answer was, "I know John, now come to bed." I often regretted later that I didn't react with a sweet comment.

Our very last trip was a cruise through the Panama Canal, starting in Fort Lauderdale and ending up in San Francisco—home. We celebrated his 83rd birthday on board. Only a few times did his actions indicate irregular behavior patterns. Few people realized anything was wrong.

We enjoyed a wonderful dinner together on Father's Day at one of his favorite steak houses. And then came July 4th. For years, John had joined the veterans on a VFW float in Danville's annual Independence Day parade. This year was no exception. Though he had a nasty fall early in the morning he insisted on going to the parade.

Two hours later I got a call form one of his friends: "You better come pick John up right away. There's something wrong." After I managed to wind my way through police barricades his friends more or less carried him into the car. He slept all afternoon. The next morning he was unable to get out of bed. With the help of Luke and one of his friends, we put him in my car and took him to the hospital.

That's where the real nightmare began. John would have said, "I went to hell in a wheelbarrow." He had often declared, "Hospitals will kill you." If he had only known. Up until his hospital admittance I had been in charge of all his medications, making sure that the pills he took for one ailment did not aggravate another. Now it was completely taken out of my hands.

His recent fall was not the main problem; he had a very high fever and was soon diagnosed with a blood infection. Each morning a different doctor tended to him, each of them changing medications as they thought best. There was little coordination between doctors. When I noticed how much heart medication he was given, I immediately asked for a lower dose, as I knew it would lower his—already low—blood pressure to the point where he would faint or fall. The cardiologist adjusted the dose. The next day a different cardiologist was on duty, who upped the dose again. Worse, they made assumptions. "He has heart disease? Then he must have high cholesterol." Cholesterol-lowering drugs were given in spite of my assurance that his level was far below normal. Each day brought new intolerable surprises.

I visited with John twice a day, trying to be cheerful, hiding my frustrations, acting as if nothing was wrong. I didn't know how much he understood about his condition and was afraid I might upset him talking about it. Once while waiting downstairs I had a conversation with a Catholic priest. "Would you like for me to visit your husband?" he asked. I declined his offer, not only because John wasn't Catholic, but I was afraid a visit from a priest would make him think he was dying. Later I thought I should have let him visit, that John might have enjoyed talking to a man of God. Joyce told me after John died what he had said to her in the hospital: "I don't think your mother knows how sick I really am." Should I have acted differently? How did I know what was the right or wrong thing to do?

After a three-week stay at John Muir Hospital he went briefly into a private nursing home until other arrangements could be made. When I contacted the VA Hospital in Livermore—a thirty-five minute drive from Danville—I was told John had top priority for admittance to its nursing home: a combat veteran and ex-POW with 100% disability rating. John took his last ride through familiar territory and the countryside leading to the beautiful facility.

He liked his stay at once and seemed pleased to have so many veterans around him. At times he thought he was on vacation. "Would you take me back to the hotel room?" he asked after I had been pushing him around in his wheelchair. Another time he said to me, "I feel so sorry for all these old and sick guys." That statement baffled me at first until I remembered that twelve years earlier he had been a volunteer at that same place, entertaining the sick and dying veterans and helping them get around. He must have thought for a brief moment that he was back doing volunteer work.

Occasionally his mind was remarkably clear. One day, because of a rash on my left ring finger, I had switched my rings to my right hand. John noticed right away. "Where is your wedding ring?" he asked. To the very end, he always recognized me, as well as Luke and Joyce. When my brother visited from Holland and accompanied me, John looked at him and said, "Well, I'll be, look who's here." But trying to play a game of checkers with him, he had no idea what to do.

Since the beginning of John's illness the veterans and other long-time friends had been visiting him regularly. One day a large group of veterans met in the dining hall of the nursing home, discussing the fate of the Livermore VA hospital. John and I happened to sit close to the entry hall when they filed out. Upon seeing John, all his old friends immediately gathered around him, making him feel as if he was part of the coffee group again. It was truly a great farewell party.

Two weeks into his stay he suddenly took a turn for the worse. His physical therapist told me he could no longer follow directions. He was moved "upstairs," to a section with the sickest patients. We all knew what that meant: "terminal patients."

Visiting was heart-wrenching; I tried to talk to him and feed him ice cream, and other treats I knew he liked, but there was very little response.

On September 20, I called his nurse early in the morning, as usual, to see how John was doing. "He's really lucid today," she told me. I rushed right over. He was sitting in his wheelchair in the activity room, *looking at a newspaper.* His face brightened when he saw me. I gave him a big hug and said, "I love you, hon." He looked back at me with those twinkling blue eyes and said very clearly, "I love you too." Those were the last words we spoke to each other—it was our final goodbye. Shortly after, his breathing became distressed and he was taken away for treatment. The next day he was in a semi-coma.

Luke, Joyce and I had a long discussion with John's doctor, a very caring woman. In addition to not being able to swallow anymore, John had developed pneumonia and his organs were beginning to shut down. Years earlier John had signed a health directive, which included not wanting to be kept alive as a vegetable. Consequently we opted out of a feeding tube. Though we knew it would have been John's wish and the only humane thing to do, it was still a hard decision to make.

On the 23rd the three of us gathered around him early, trying to make him as comfortable as possible. After a brief lunch across the street at Wente's winery we returned to his bedside. We left him late in the afternoon, planning to return early the next morning.

On a whim Luke decided to take his family back to John that night: "Let's go see Opa." They arrived at 9:30. Five minutes later, after saying a prayer and holding his hand, John died. I wish I could have been there, but was glad he didn't die alone.

The following days went by in a frenzy with arrangements for cremation and a memorial service. Luke and Mary Ellen took charge of everything. In a short time they put together a video about John's life and arranged the entire memorial service in the Veterans Hall in Danville.

My whole family spoke: Luke first, then Joyce and the grandchildren. Martine read a beautiful bible verse, while Emily, Megan and Dalton read a script they had written themselves about their Opa they so adored. Tributes to John were paid by two of the veterans, as well as the son of John's best POW buddy *Charlie* from Texas.

There was a color guard, flag folding with presentation and a bugler playing taps. The singing of the Marine Corps hymn brought the memorial service to a close. John would have been proud. Six months later his ashes were interred with military honors at Arlington National Cemetery. Joyce, Luke, Dalton, and I attended the ceremony, as well as John's best Marine Corps friend from Danville.

Two months after his death a two-page article about John's life—"A Local Hero Remembered"—appeared in the "Valley Citizen," a magazine of the San Ramon Valley.

The following year the veterans, as a tribute to John, installed a large photograph of him—in uniform, taken in 1949—with a plaque listing his accomplishments, in the Danville Veterans Hall.

I recently read a quote attributed to Ralph Waldo Emerson: "To share often and much…to know even one life has breathed easier because you have lived; this is to have succeeded."

Well, John, I concluded, *you* have succeeded.

John's photograph in the Veterans Hall in Danville.

CHAPTER 51

Going It Alone

For years, I had known the time would come when I would have to live on alone without John. I was not a "helpless widow," like some of my friends who had no clue about financial matters and were afraid to drive by themselves after their husbands died. John had been glad to let me do the check writing, income tax preparation, and investing. He also left the planning for our many trips entirely up to me. Nothing changed there.

But...I felt so *alone*. After sharing your life for over fifty years with another human being it comes as a shock when that abruptly comes to an end. I thought I had prepared myself to be without John, especially towards the end when his mind was deteriorating at an alarming speed. It had devastated me to see this once proud man be reduced to a shadow of himself. I know *he* would not have wanted to continue living like that.

So I expected to be relieved when it was all over. And yes, on the one hand I was relieved, for *him*. I knew he was now in a better place. So why couldn't I be happy that we had each other for so long, much longer than either of us expected? But I missed our life together, especially our life before the later phases of Alzheimer's. I missed having someone to share my thoughts with, to reminisce and laugh with. I missed holding his hand. *I am no longer the most important person in anyone's life,* was a devastating realization.

Over the next few months I went through several phases. Guilt played a role: Was I always nice enough to him? Had I appreciated him enough? I felt guilty for having criticized him when he dressed in clothes that didn't match, and for buying hats at all sorts of military gatherings.

Then came regrets: had I taken our life together too much for granted? Had I experienced all the good things in our married life intensely enough? At times, tears were just streaming down my face.

My children tried to help, telling me to be more realistic: "Mom, nobody is perfect. You made Dad happy, you have wonderful memories and you always did the best you could under the circumstances."

I treasured some of the condolence letters I received, expressing appreciation for the man John had been. "John's passing is as if a giant sequoia has fallen—he was a giant in our modest world and a tower of strength in the veteran's community, upholding the principles we all, especially Marines, adhere to. His valor, patriotism, love of family, friends, and life is an example for all of us." From another friend: "What can I say when we lose a great man! I will always miss our personal talks and his history lessons on WWII. John was a unique Marine to all of us. He never quit trying to make things better for his family and friends. He always talked about and praised you for your love and as he would say, 'She's so smart, knows so many languages and is a very good business woman,' with a big smile on his face!"

Those letters really touched my heart. It made me proud to read the veterans' reactions to his death; how they had admired and valued him. Moreover, I found it incredibly sweet that John, at his age, would still brag about me to his friends.

CHAPTER 52

Letters and Pictures

I started writing letters to my family and in particular my mother from the moment I arrived in Portugal in December of 1949. They usually consisted of two densely spaced typewritten pages, at least one letter a week. They described all my daily experiences and adventures in great detail. Several years before her death she said to me, "Why don't you take the letters home with you? If I would suddenly die they might be accidentally tossed."

So I had had them in my possession since the middle of the eighties. I had leafed through them a few times, searching for pages telling about the time our children were little, sharing with John some of the cute things they had said and done. Nothing more. I stored them in a safe place.

In desperate need of any kind of emotional support to help me cope with John's death I thought, what better way to feel him near me than reading the letters about our life? I started to read from the very beginning, each and every one of them. I simply couldn't stop. Our life started to unfold before my eyes, like a motion picture. My first meeting with John, our first date. Though I had of course omitted any kind of intimate details I could fill those images in very well.

For days I kept on reading. I relived John's kindness and unselfishness, the exhilaration around the birth of our children, the excitement about a diamond ring from the PX, the work we put in together in our new homes, our store, and the trips we made as a family. What a partnership we had been, what a team, encouraging each other in our endeavors.

An amazing thing happened: *I fell in love all over again.* Oh John, I thought, why didn't I read the letters long before, how we could have enjoyed reliving our life together, reminiscing. I desperately wanted a sign. I wanted John to tell me, "It's okay honey, don't cry, I understand."

I started to toss old magazines, stacks and stacks of them. John had always loved the Reader's Digest with all its funny jokes. I found hundreds of old copies. Before putting them in the trash I decided to leaf through them. I chuckled at jokes we had enjoyed together and re-read short stories we had discussed. Then suddenly I came upon a poem I had never seen before, written almost one hundred years ago. I knew with all my heart it was John's message to me, the encouragement I had been waiting for. It said:

Death is nothing at all.

I have only slipped away into the next room, I am I, and you are you,
Whatever we were to each other, that we are still.
Call me by the old familiar name, speak of me in the easy way, which you always used.
Put no difference into your tone. Wear no forced air of solemnity or sorrow.
Laugh as we always laughed at the little jokes that we enjoyed together.
Play, smile, think of me, pray for me.
Let my name be ever the household word that it always was.
Let it be spoken without an effort, without the ghost of a shadow upon it.
Life means all that it ever meant. It is the same as it ever was.

There is absolute and unbroken continuity. What is death but a negligible accident?
Why should I be out of mind because I am out of sight? I am but waiting for you for an interval, somewhere very near, just around the corner. All is well.

"Thank you, John," I whispered.

While continuing to read the letters I came upon the year 1965: *Toto's death.* Though in my state of mind I didn't really want to hear about more sadness, I felt drawn to relive that part of my life. Maybe this was all meant to be. I had totally forgotten what I had sent my parents to help with their grief: the Catherine Marshall books. Could they help *me* now, I wondered. Between second-hand bookstores and the library I found them all. The most thought provoking was titled: "To Live Again." I devoured the book and craved for more. I learned how to pray for strength, how to cope. I re-joined the Methodist Church.

In the meantime I had started gathering pictures of our life. We had about a dozen different photo albums, some picturing special events, others about travel, a lot with just buildings or landscapes, and people I vaguely remembered. I decided to make one big album depicting our life. This was good therapy. I started with our photos from Portugal, then our wedding, and the birth of our children. How grateful I was John had been such an avid photographer!

When I finished with the old albums I looked at the many thousands of color slides John had made. Yes, I tossed hundreds of them that were of no interest to me, like the slides he had bought at museums and historical sights. I was only interested in the ones *we*, our family, appeared in. Not long after I sorted through them I discovered that slides could be made into a DVD. I picked the best five hundred and now have an hour-long DVD with pictures made from 1950, when we first met, through 1972. Luke and Joyce were thrilled with these new details of their childhood.

Next I made an album about John's life as a Marine. Very recently Luke discovered a DVD with scenes of the liberation of John's prison camp. To our amazement and delight *John appeared in it.* Luke made stills for the album. I also added copies of numerous newspaper articles with John as subject, and articles in various local magazines after his death.

Wanting to hear John's voice again, I looked at the videos made of talks he gave to groups about his POW experiences. What follows needs a prologue: In addition to his many cute, short and snappy jokes John told one long, drawn out joke that I detested. "It's way too long," I often told him, "You keep on telling it just to get my goat." Whenever the occasion arose, in new groups, who hadn't heard the joke before, he would tell it again, embellishing it and, to my horror, lengthen it. The joke required a lot of hand movements and facial distortions. There was a moral to the story: "the importance of a college education." Once I told him, "John, if I hear that joke one more time I'm going to scream."

So here I was listening to his speech, taped during one of his visits to Bonifay, to a group of Adult Education students. Before he talked about his POW experiences he told the group how proud he was that they wanted to better themselves. "Let me tell you a joke about education," he continued. That's when I knew what was coming. I sat watching the screen, in utter fascination, hearing the once hated story again, enjoying every minute of it. "John, you devil," I shouted out, "You got me again!"

EPILOGUE

It's been over four years since John died. Though I have learned to cope with being alone and have come to enjoy some of the aspects of my "new" life, there's not one hour of the day I don't think about him, missing him. Dreary days are the worst. Alone in the house on a rainy afternoon I want to hear John say, "You make the tea, I'll build a fire." "Build" meaning lighting a match to the gas logs in the fireplace.

I treasure all the good memories of our life together and I know he's still near me trying to make me happy. A year after John died, after fifty long years of struggling with perms I suddenly got natural curl back in my hair. Try as you might to explain it medically, to me it meant a gift from John, saying, "I know how much your curly hair meant to you, here's a present from me."

There have been times I started feeling sorry for myself. But immediately after, I thought, what did you expect? Nothing lasts forever, count your blessings, you've had a long, wonderful life, and still have so much to be grateful for. If you hadn't been within five minutes from the hospital when John had his massive heart attack you would have lost him twenty-five years earlier.

My children and grandchildren all try to make me happy. I can always count on them. Their chatter and laughter often fill my house. My church has also been a tremendous support to me. I've made many new friends and have come to appreciate old friends more than before. At times I reminisce with John's veteran buddies—the coffee group—who loved and respected him. One particular observation really touched me: "If you didn't like John, there had to be something wrong with you."

It's funny how some little things irk me. Whenever I have to fill in a form with boxes to mark your marital status it bugs me when only three choices are given: single, married, or divorced. Hey, I'm not single; John is still part of me! I then draw a fourth box and fill in *widow*.

I feel very sentimental about John's possessions. His beloved Volvo wagon stayed parked next to the house for years. When my youngest granddaughter Martine got her driver's license I gave it to her, to keep it in the family. John would have approved of that. Martine told me a while ago, "I feel safe driving Opa's car, as if he's there with me, protecting me, like a guardian angel."

John's desk, surrounded by lots of Marine Corps paraphernalia, medals and ribbons, remains unchanged. I gave his favorite Marine Corps jacket to his best Marine buddy from the coffee group. As for the rest of his clothes, it took me a long time before I could part with any of them. After two years I packed up a number of bags full to donate to a Veterans hospital. But even now I still can't part with some of the shirts and jackets he liked best. They will probably be hanging in my closet forever.

Some of my friends have voiced their surprise that I continue living by myself in such a big house. I would not *dream* of ever leaving. The house is filled with memories of our thirty-four years of living here together. Everywhere I look I see John, feel his presence. When I look out of the window and see the mountain we both loved so much, *our* Mount Diablo, I feel content. My children know: I want to live here till I die.

About six months after John's death I knew I had to find new ways to fill my days. I was long finished with the photo albums/scrapbooks about our life and had read *the letters* my mother kept at least three times. In addition to my church activities and other volunteer work, I joined several bridge groups. As I hadn't played the game in fifty years, I bought books on new methods and conventions. Bridge was one way to keep my brain active. After seeing what it had done to John, I had become deathly afraid of Alzheimer's or any other form of dementia. Genetically speaking, I have a fifty/fifty chance of getting the disease, so I wanted to increase my odds against it. For years I had been an avid crossword puzzle solver. Now I found other puzzles to work on and have become what you might call a Sudoku junkie.

In January of 2005 I flew to Washington DC to visit John's grave in Arlington. From there I took a plane to Charleston SC, rented a car, and drove to Beaufort to visit our old stomping grounds. What a difference fifty years make! This time I viewed the town as a lovely old place with beautiful southern mansions, big oak trees with Spanish moss, and, at the water's edge, a lively marina. I drove by our old house, now surrounded by many tall trees. In my mind I saw our children playing in the yard and John tending to his watermelons. (No *gnats*—it was winter.)

After giving talks to several groups about my experiences in Holland under Nazi occupation people started to encourage me to write a book. A little hesitant at first, words soon began pouring from my laptop, combining my story with John's experiences, culminating in our life together.

First I translated from Dutch the pertinent facts from the letters I wrote my mother, picking and choosing only the most interesting parts. A very time-consuming task, as there are close to *twenty-five hundred* of them. Next I scoured through all John's papers, partly finished manuscripts, and letters to and from friends.

When I came to the end of my writing I wasn't satisfied with the result; it was in precise chronological order, telling what happened during each month of each year. I found the finished product too boring, too drawn out. My manuscript lay dormant for almost two years.

At church one Sunday, I ran into a couple who mentioned that *Harry*, a 91 year-old man John and I had known over thirty years ago, had written a book about his life, consisting of funny and interesting "vignettes." As I showed a real interest and told them about my efforts, they brought me a copy.

After reading Harry's book, I knew I had found the solution to telling our story: combine it with anecdotes about special people and events in our life. The book you just read became the result.

Thanksgiving 2007—surrounded by the grandchildren:
l. to r. Dalton, Megan, Emily, Martine

With Luke and Joyce—Christmas 2006

Printed in the United States
119010LV00004B/106-999/P

9 781600 472244